AF579985

LIMITED EDITION PHOTOGRAPHS

How to Produce and Market Your Own

By William R. Eastman III

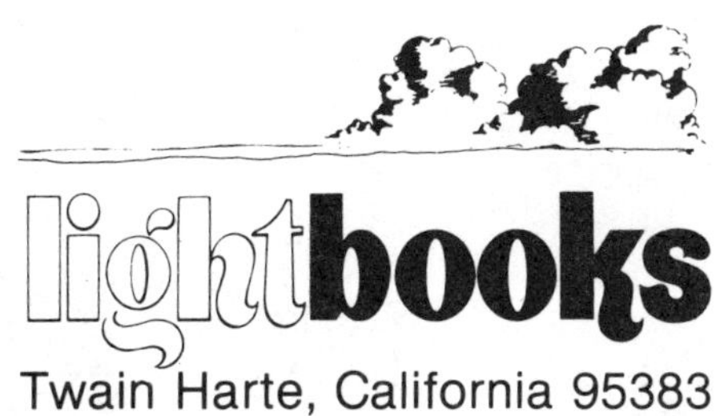

Second Edition

Published by LIGHTBOOKS
P. O. Box 1268
Twain Harte, California 95383

ISBN: 0-934420-02-5
LCCCN: 80-84694

TABLE OF CONTENTS

FOREWORD

It's a satisfying experience seeing your work hanging on the wall of a fine gallery or a bank, a doctor's office, commercial building, or even a private residence. Producing some of your better images in the form of photo art is rewarding in many ways. Above everything else, it can be a very profitable outlet for your long years of patience and hard work.

In the following pages we will be discussing primarily Limited Edition prints – how to produce them, how to market them. This book is meant to be a guide to the beginner. At the same time it was written as a solid think piece for those of you who have already seen the obvious market for your photography in the form of prints.

Although Limited Editions are the main function of this book, I wish to point out that we are in no way limiting its usefulness to this restricted art form. There will be many times when it will be to your advantage to sign – but not limit – your prints. There are strong markets for display and decorator prints which should not be limited. I will discuss as many of these areas as possible.

Most important, keep in mind that the marketing and advertising techniques which apply to Limited Edition prints, will be just as effective in the sale of display and decorator prints.

The major difference between Limited Edition prints and other art prints is price and volume. There are strong markets for both. Learning the difference and making the most effective use of your photo art is what this book is all about.

Since the first publication of this book, Photographic Art has made major strides to become an acceptable, demanded medium. Photographic Art specialty stores have opened in many large and mid-sized market areas.

Surely, there is no better time to make a push for your own photographic art. Do it with style and class – and good luck!

William R. Eastman III

I dedicate this book to my wife, Jeri,
and to the man who made it all possible —
George Eastman.

SECTION I

THE UNIVERSAL IMAGE

The demand and sales potential of art begins with the recognition of a universal image. The quality with which art is produced, its appeal and uniqueness are all factors in its value and mortality as art. It should make little difference whether this final form of expression is produced in oil, bronze, silkscreen, watercolor, or a photographic print. As long as its appeal is universal and powerful and its quality is the finest the artist can produce, it is art and must be recognized as such.

In the past there have been many holdouts among collectors and art buyers towards the recognition of photographic art. The art world has been geared to lithographs, woodcuts and silkscreens. Many still view photography as nothing more than machine-produced images which require little talent, artistic merit, involvement or insight.

In the majority of cases these strongholds of old world art forms are wrong. They have been influenced not only by the standard recognized art forms, but also by what we might refer to as the Kodak-Polaroid myth. In a miracle of mass-marketing, these two companies have brought photography and instant throw-away art into every home in America. Nearly eveyone who owns or has access to a Polaroid or Instamatic secretly considers himself a photographer. Commercial and Portrait photographs have recognized this problem for a long time. Because of the public's access to cheap prints made possible by mass-production machine printing, it has been very difficult to convince or educate the public to the actual physical cost and value involved in quality photography. Indeed, pricing on any aspect of quality photography or art print sales is the first major hurdle to overcome.

PHOTOGRAPHIC ART COMES OF AGE

A recent edition of Kodak's Studio Light was devoted almost exclusively to a discussion involving the sudden rise and acceptance of photographic art. This publication, which is produced for professional photographers in the United States and Canada, indicates a major push by Kodak to get photographic art in front of the public and to the eyes of architects, interior designers, and professional art dealers.

Sherman Emery, editor of the presitigous Interior Design magazine, is quoted as saying: "The full potential of this art form has only just begun to be realized . . . its further development lies not only in the hands of creative photographers but on the drawing boards of creative architects and designers."

Another professional in the field, Richard W. Jones, past president of the American Society of Interior Designers, is quoted by Kodak: "As a professional interior designer, with 25 years of experience in the field, I can honestly say that at last there is an art form for designers, their clients and others to use that is as adaptable to its many uses as it is available. I salute the coming of the age of photographic art as an intrinsic element of and for interior design." (Both quotes are from Studio Light for February, 1978.

More proof of these statements is showing up locally all around us. Not only is photography being accepted by interior designers and architects as a tool in their various enterprises, but it is being accepted by industry and other commercial enterprises with a zest that can only be described as incredible.

In the process of marketing my own selection of art prints and limited edition prints, I found demand and hidden markets virtually everywhere. Doctors and other professional people (accountants, lawyers, dentists, business executives and a multitude of others) proved to be eager clients for photographic art. About 70% of these sales ended up on the walls of their offices, while the remainder went home for the dens or the wives. Other markets are booming as large companies build new offices and need artwork to decorate them and liven them up. Banks remain a major outlet, as do hospitals and restaurants. Many smaller businesses and mall shopping centers can be enticed into using photographic art and commercial photography to stop crowds and draw customers into their stores.

Photography is an affordable art. In many cases it should be promoted as such and work should be sold on its own merit and appeal, not because of its eventual potential art value.

The art market that is now opening its arms to photographic art will be receptive as long as photographers sell their work with the same professionalism, discretion, honesty and quality that has become the hallmark of other forms of art.

IS THERE AN ART MARKET FOR YOUR PHOTOGRAPHY?

If you are a serious photographer, if you have a unique viewpoint on the world, if you are willing to take time in advance to organize and prepare only the best of your work for sale, and if you are honest with yourself and are able to price your work competitively according to its realistic value, then the answer to the question is an absolute yes! Yes! YES!

As photographers we are judged exclusively by what people see. If they are allowed to see only our best work we are judged as professionals, and our talents and skills are rewarded accordingly. This means very simply that the majority of your work should be locked away in your files – where it is useful as reference for you – but not seen by the public.

If you are like me, you may shoot anywhere from one to a dozen rolls of film before you come up with exactly the right image of any particular subject or assignment. I'm being very honest when I admit that I bracket like crazy, even when I know exactly what exposure I want. I learned a long time ago that the only place to judge your photographic ideas is on the light table. How many times have you looked at that final, hard-won slide and said to yourself: "If I had just been another stop under or . . ."

You know what I'm talking about. Even with the increasing price of photography and supplies, film is still the cheapest item and there is nothing in the world more frustrating or lonely than flying three thousand miles to get a photograph – then miss it because you tried to economize on film. Any photographer that considers himself a Robin Hood is only fooling himself. One arrow might have been enough for the man in green but it falls short for the serious professional photographer. Personally, I have learned more from the mistakes I've made by shooting extra footage and experimenting with every shot than I have from all the articles, advice and classes available to me over the years. Pay attention to your shots but remain loose and flexible. If it does not improve your photography it will at least make you an expert at hitting the garbage basket with a dud slide from twenty paces.

The important point is to keep and show only the best work you are capable of doing. What gives each of us a fair shot at the art market in photography today is our own individual outlook and perspective on the world as we see it. It is this special way that each of us observes our subject and portrays it on film that makes us unique and makes our work interesting and salable to the public.

The diversity of your work will have a lot to do with your success in the art market. To begin, you should probably have on hand at least two hundred strong images. Among these there are probably eight or ten shots that are powerful and unique enough to be considered for a line of Limited Editions. The remainder can be sold in any quantity as decorator and designer prints to offices, banks, etc.

In the majority of cases it is to your advantage to shoot slides. As you will see in the section on marketing, slides are an excellent way to show a potential client a wide selection of your work. Secondly, a slide gives you an absolute original whether you are printing it yourself or sending it to a good lab. There can be no doubt as to color balance, sharpness, or saturation. The biggest advantage of slides is that they are what the majority of art directors and publishers require if any of your work is to be published in full color. Getting your work published is one of the photo-artist's primary goals. It gets your name and talent in front of the public and it gives you another profit outlet for your photography.

If you are a dyed-in-the-wool negative man, then you should stick with it. It will end up costing you more to get prints ready for displays and private presentations, but it is probably not worthwhile to change your style and work methods just to go along with the crowd. It is more important to do what you know best and what is more comfortable for you.

WHAT TYPES OF PHOTOS SELL?

Once again, virtually every good photo has a potential market. There will always be some that sell better than others. Diversity and versatility are still the key. You will have some clients who want only abstracts. Others will want portraits, scenics, industry, close-ups, or almost anything. You are probably very good with one type or style of photography. This is still where you should spend the majority of your time and effort. If your forte is close-ups or nature, stick to it. Do what you are good at first and hardest, then diversify a percentage of your work so that there will be something to appeal to just about everyone.

LANDSCAPES, NATURE

Landscapes and nature photography still dominate sales for their universal appeal. Whenever people are surrounded by walls or cities, they begin to fantasize about far-away places and the simple life. These are the kind of people who like to fill their walls with animals and scenics — flowers, rocks, sunsets and open spaces. Ideas for this type of photography are virtually unlimited. With a wide angle, a close-up, and a zoom you could shoot for days in a single area without overlapping ideas or content. The secret here is to isolate your subjects and keep them simple for greatest impact.

CLOSE-UPS. Blades of grass at all seasons, leaves, insects, mammals, reptiles; photomacrography of virtually anything, no matter how abstract; ponds, deserts, forests, mountains, oceans, beaches, parks — you name it and you will find a multitude of subjects for the close-up lens.

Before you shoot, ask yourself the question: "Does it appeal to me?" If it does, chances are it will appeal to others.

NATURE. All animals — especially the young — have a strong appeal. Again, isolate them or show them in the grandeur of their environment. Horses always sell and all other wild things. Pets seldom. Zoos are good and have easy access if you avoid identifying backgrounds.

LANDSCAPES. Old buildings, seasons, areas with vast space, mountains, forests, sunsets, seascapes, deserts, and a thousand more. Watch for dramatic lighting, simplicity and appeal. Use depth of field to get unique viewpoints on the ordinary.

STORMS. There's more beauty in a blizzard or electrical storm than one would suspect. This kind of drama always sells but it is very hard to capture. Look for fog, snow, rain, lightning, and all the other perils of nature. They are the winners.

ABSTRACTS

Another growing market is for abstract photography. The winners here are anything with strong graphic designs, dramatic lighting, or items of curiosity. This is where technology and the joy of experimenting can make you a winner. Dig into the back issues of the photo magazines and you will find hundreds of ways to make abstract photography with filters, chemistry and clever gimmicks. The object is not to con your viewer, but to appeal to his sense of curiosity and joy of the extraordinary.

Our world has produced several incredible abstract artists in all art mediums, including photography. With the proper perseverence and marketing techniques, a good abstract photographer can make a fortune. The competition in this area is small in comparison to other photographic subjects, and there is a huge, untapped market for the prints. It is kind of like the unknown millions of us who secretly read fantasy books and patiently waited for a STAR WARS to be produced. If you get on it and do it right, the buyers will appear out of the woodwork.

SPORTS

Of course there is a market for sports photography. It has all the elements — universal appeal, drama, beauty of motion, etc. But a word of caution: The great photographers have already been here and cheap posters abound everywhere. Your market is going to be limited by any number of things, and your work had better be very good. If you want to shoot some sports to round out your selection, I would suggest several things. Try not to date your photos. Clothing and technology are the villains here. In team sports uniforms that are recognizable symbols of specific teams can limit your market potential except in specific local areas. Abstracts, slow shutter speed action shots, and personal drama photos are probably your best bets.

INDUSTRIAL AND COMMERCIAL PHOTOGRAPHS

Your best bet here, of course, is to hit the oil company or railroad at its executive offices. Show them samples of what you have done before and sell them on the idea of an in-depth photo presentation on all the aspects of their particular industry. There is an extremely healthy market here. Corporate offices — especially those away from the action — love nothing better than dramatic photos of their products and employees in action. There are thousands of different types of industries you can approach — steel mills, forestry products, computer systems, banks, fisheries, airlines, and multitudes of others. Even if you are in a small town, there is bound to be one or two special industries that would love to have a personal-approach photographer document the business that dominates their lives. Remember one thing: in most cases this will be a one-shot assignment so you will need a lot of good photos of all aspects of the business. There will be no royalties down the road as with your other lines of art prints. You should price yourself accordingly, but not out of the market. One happy client can mean thousands of dollars in additional business from his friends down the road.

TRAVEL

Little needs to be said here, mainly because the kind of scenes you shoot in any particular country are going to be much the same. The uniqueness of the area and its people, wildlife, and environment are going to give you a bonus for unique, exotic photos. Again, don't date them, keep them simple, and above all don't take tourist snapshots. Select an angle or a technique that will make your photos different and more dramatic or appealing than all the rest. The best thing about travel is that it gets you away from all the sameness that you have around home. You will see and shoot things that are commonplace to the inhabitants but are new and wonderful to you. If you keep these things in perspective you will come home with winners and add a lot of depth to your files.

PORTRAITURE

Wanting to be a photographer and having to put bread on the table at the same time, has produced some incredible portrait photographers. These people are artists and artesans at the same time. And, yes, there is also a market for portrait-type art if it is unique and dramatic. The biggest drawbacks are that people are recognizable and often dated. To find a universal image here you must be clever and unique. The winners here are famous people, different nationalities and races, and of course, beautiful women, or people whose faces have been weathered by their environment and occupations. Some portrait-type work is good in any portfolio. The caution again is that if you want the backbone of your art presentation to be portraits, you had better be very good because the competition is steep.

EROTIC AND EXOTIC

There will always be a market for tasteful nudes. The beauty of the human body is universal and immortal. No other medium offers the artist such an opportunity to create a diversity of moods and expressions in the human drama as photography.

In the area of the exotic we can include everything from aerial photos to underwater photography. Anything that is unique from the point of view of perspective or environment will fit into the exotic section of your portfolio. Exotic photos sell because of their perspective and their ability to take someone into another world at a glance.

ASSIGNMENT: PHOTO ART

Nearly all successful professional photographers approach each and every photo project as an assignment. The photo stories in newspapers and magazines are a prime example of this. They illustrate any particular incident from as many aspects and angles as possible. A good fire feature will show the blaze, human interest around the area, the firemen at work, someone getting medical treatment; anything at all related to the fire. A series of different lenses, filters, and perspective will be used to give a dramatic and interesting insight into each of the various dramas taking place.

The photo artist must do the same. Even when you are just relaxing on a Sunday with your camera, it will help if you secretly consider yourself on an assignment. Imagine that there are twenty other photographers working around you – all of them shooting the same thing you are – and the guy with the best photos gets the account, or the agency job, or the color spread in Sports Illustrated. Give yourself some competition. It will sharpen your eye and help you find the shots that are out of the ordinary.

LIMITED EDITIONS: ARE THEY FOR YOU?

As we have discussed, there is a marketplace for photographic art. Nearly everything you sell should be signed and matted. The majority of your work will sell at competitive prices and you will attempt to sell as many prints of any particular image as possible. The more prints you sell, the less expensive each individual print will be to produce and the more money you will make. Also, by selling your prints in volume, you will be able to expose more and more people to yourself and your photography.

But out of every hundred of your best prints will be an image so special — so unique and powerful — that you might want to keep it apart from the others. You might want to restrict sales so that it will not become commonplace or trite.

Thus the question arises; should you go to all of the extra expense and trouble of producing and promoting a line of limited edition photographs? What are they anyway? What makes them worth so much more? Why are they worth the bother?

Limited Edition or 'original' prints have been officially recognized for centuries as a rewarding and acceptable way for artists to produce their work. Today, with speculators and investors looking for another way to keep pace with inflation, original prints are becoming a solid market and prices are at a premium. Woodcuts and lithographs by the old masters have been known to sell for thousands of dollars, while the work of many recent artists often appreciates from 30% to 90% a year.

In the past owning original art has been reserved for the very few, mostly the wealthy. During the past decade, public awareness and the availability of 'affordable' art has changed this a great deal. Also to be credited are a lot of unique marketing techniques such as direct mail, airport booths, gift catalogues and art magazines that have both educated the public and created a demand for limited edition art.

What exactly is a limited edition or original print?

To begin with, experts set several consistent qualifications. An original is a print that has been pulled by various methods directly from an artist's master — be it a litho plate, a woodcut, or — in the case of photography — a transparency or negative. Further, an original print is printed under the artist's supervision. It must be signed and — if limited — numbered by him.

For example, I might sign the first print in a limited edition of fifty prints: WILLIAM R. EASTMAN III 1/50. In fact, I like to give each image a number and the date it was taken. Hence, I would sign an image like the Flying Dutchman:

WILLIAM R. EASTMAN III
1001 Nov. 74 1/50

Art dealers and experts also prefer that the artist sign in pencil. We will discuss the actual signing in the next section.

Another thing experts demand of limited editions is that the artist's master be destroyed after the edition has been printed. In such a way the buyer is protected from the artist, or someone else, who might pull additional, illegal prints. We will also discuss this further in a later section.

The value of any limited edition print lies in its strong supply-demand orientation. As an artist and his work become accepted and desired by the public, demand for his best paintings, etchings, or photographs is bound to increase.

If over the next five to ten years your art prints were to be sold widely, if your name were to become well known, if you were to receive the kind of national attention and recognition that many other modern artists have received, your work would suddenly not only be in demand, but worth more.

Let's say, for example, that your most famous image was printed in a limited edition of 100. Suddenly, about 500 people across the country wish they could buy it and would have done so at the original price. But of these only about 150 are very serious about owning that photograph. When they start bidding on your print, the price will be controlled only by their willingness to pay and their desire to own.

In simple words, you would have a rarity on your hands. Like the stamp or coin that is one of a kind, your print would be valuable not only for its beauty and worth as art, but for the fact that there are only so many left and, as such, they have a value in their own right.

A limited edition print, properly done, is the most discriminating and profitable way that you can bring your work to the attention of the public. Again, it must consist of only your finest work, with all the frills, printed and mounted with the utmost quality you or your lab is capable of.

As you will see in the next section, there are hassles and problems connected with printing limited editions. Chances are very slim that you will ever be taken to court over one of your regular art prints, nor will the problem of forgeries give you much concern. But these and other problems might well be expected if you don't take the proper precautions in the production and marketing of a line of limited editions.

If you release an image in a limited edition of 300 prints, then there damn well better be only 300 prints on the market and you had better be able to prove it. When your work starts being worth money — big money — people will be tempted to do anything they can to copy it and/or find a way to get back at you for the profits. For this reason you must be extra cautious with your limited editions. They are time consuming and, in many cases, they are a speculation. If you make the mistake of printing an entire edition before you have a market for them, you could very well end up with a thousand dollars worth of worthless prints on your hands.

Enough of the negative aspect. It does exist as with any business enterprise. Knowing that it is there can help guide you in your various decisions. As to whether or not you should consider a line of limited editions, my answer is a cautious yes. Your very best work deserves to appreciate in value. It deserves the attention and respect that it can receive through limited editions. If you are going to work seriously at producing photo art for sale, you are only reaching part of the market and prestige available unless you have several limited editions in your portfolio. Read on and then decide for yourself. I will give you every angle I can to help you make your prints a success.

SECTION II

YOUR LAB OR YOU?

The cold hard fact of the matter is that your prints will be more valuable years down the road if you print them yourself. The reasoning behind this is due mostly to love and tradition. The artist traditionally produces his work out of love and sweat and blood. When such an artist puts his signature on the completed masterpiece, it's his way of saying, "This is the best I can do. I have signed my name here because I am satisfied that this work is representative of my skills and talents."

In most art forms the artist *must* be involved through the final production if the work is to be his at all. Photography, on the other hand, is one of those areas of art where the 'original' image is produced within the camera. The reproduction of that image does not at all require its creator once the original has been produced. In fact, because of the very high cost of a good custom color lab and because of the specialized technical skills required, it is often to the advantage of the photographer and his final reproductions to use a highly specialized custom lab rather than attempt to do the work himself. On the other hand, if a photographer allows anyone else to print his originals for him, he must exercise absolute rule over the prints produced. If the photographer is not at least 100% satisfied with the final results, the prints should be destroyed and reprinted.

When it comes to black and white, I have every confidence that I can print exactly what I want and there's no way I want someone else messing with my negatives. The equipment I need to do top quality work is reasonably priced and highly portable, I can take it where I want to go and control the end result.

Unfortunately, the majority of the work I produce for art prints is in color. A good color lab is not only very expensive, it is very difficult to move around at the drop of a hat. The other major problem is simply time. Color prints take time and controlled working conditions. I have neither, and I'm not alone, either. There are hundreds of photographers in exactly the same position. As working photographers we spend the majority of our time in the field on assignment or looking for the kind of subjects and conditions that will make good art prints. Consequently, it is difficult for us to print our own color.

If you are in this position, or if you simply do not have the skill to print absolutely consistent color photography, then you should seriously consider working with a quality custom lab.

I personally work with Meisel Photochrome out of Bellevue, Washington. It was difficult at first and there were some heated tempers for nearly a year. They did not want to keep my original negatives on file and I didn't want them traveling back and forth across the country. We had other problems keeping the quality and format of the prints consistent. But all of these things were eventually worked out: I can now depend on my prints being done exactly as I would do them.

If you work through a custom lab you should:

1. Make sure they have adequate facilities for storing your originals at their plant.
2. Make sure that each of your originals can be identified by an image number and description of the photo.
3. Have a strip print made, an approved sample of exactly how that photo should be printed. This includes exact color, any dodging or burning, any cropping, how it should be mounted and sprayed, or any other specifics necessary for total quality control. This strip print should remain on file with your original negatives so that the technician in charge of printing your work will know exactly what you want.
4. Work up a form that you can xerox or print up in quantity which will be sent in with each order. This form should include the detailed instructions above and specific instructions on shipping, etc. In this way there will be no excuses for foul-ups.
5. Try to work up everything in advance. Once you get into production there will simply not be time for changes or reprints.

There is one other reason you may wish to use a custom lab. If your work does become successful and you find that your volume becomes such that you simply cannot do all the work yourself, then you may be forced to consider farming out some of the less important work. If you do, don't expect anything less of your lab that you would of yourself.

A final note: If at all possible – if you have the skill and time – print your own work. It will be worth more to the public and it will be worth more to you. It is most gratifying to stick with your work from conception through production and chances are it will actually help you improve your photography.

If you must use a lab, make sure they understand what you want and make sure you are satisfied with what you get. Unless you are already a highly financed professional, it makes little sense for you to go into hock for the kind of equipment you will need to print your own photographs. Start out small and invest only what you can afford. Producing art prints can be highly rewarding and profitable, but it is like any other business – it is speculative until there is a constant demand for your work.

HOW TO SIGN YOUR WORK

Remember, your signature is your seal of approval.

All of your photography should be signed. It does not matter whether you have limited its quantity or not. Without a signature your work has about as much value as a two dollar poster.

If your photography is going to be sold in the form of prints, they should be matted. The mat board serves as a foundation for your photograph. Not only does it serve as a backing which will keep your prints from being bent and cracked, it should also be larger than the print. This will provide your print with margins, a frame beyond the actual image.

In 90% of the cases, your prints should be signed on the mat, most logically on the bottom right or left, depending both on your preference and the composition of the work. Some photographers I have seen, sign their work on the print itself only. This is up to you. You need india ink and a good drafting pen or the gold 'portrait' pens that many studios use. Personally, I feel that an art print should be signed on the mat. Traditionally, this is done in pencil. It is more personal and the most accepted in the entire art field. One of your major objectives if you are going to be successful in the art world is to give your work as much class as you can. A well matted print, discreetly signed in pencil, is one of the best ways to start.

In the case of limited editions, it is my feeling that the print should also be signed directly on the photograph. Unless you use ragboard (it is more durable and less likely to fade or stain) as your matting surface, and unless its color happens to coincide with the colors your buyers have on their walls, then the chances are that over the years your limited edition prints may be rematted for any number of reasons. Even if the rematting is done without destroying your original mat, chances are your signature might be covered up. In this case, the second signature on the print will enable your patrons to easily change mattes and frames for their purposes as styles change over the years. A second reason for signing your prints in ink will be discussed later in our section on forgery.

If you are just signing an unlimited art print, your signature in pencil on the mat will suffice. Keeping it as simple as possible will help your prints sell. If you must, you might wish to add the copyright symbol ©, followed by the date the photo was taken.

WILLIAM R. EASTMAN III © 1978

Everything you write, draw, or photograph is protected under common law copyright. As long as you can prove that you produced the work, it is protected against anyone's stealing it and calling it their own. In order to officially copyright your work you must submit a copy of the photo, publication, etc., along with the required fee to the Registrar of Copyrights. Forms and further information are available from the Registrar of Copyrights or the Library of Congress, Washington, D.C.

Many writers 'copyright' their work under common law by sending themselves a copy of their manuscript by registered mail. Such envelopes containing manuscripts are never opened but filed in a safe place. If someone later steals their work or ideas and it ends up in court, the writer can produce the registered letter to be opened by the judge. The letter has been dated and sealed from the day it was mailed. If this date was prior to when the second party published the work, it is positive proof of theft.

As a photographer you may wish to use this method. But let me warn you, sending yourself prints by registered mail can be expensive and will require a lot of storage space. Another advantage of slides is that they have the date they were processed directly on the mount. In most courts, this should be proof enough.

As I mentioned earlier, you may wish to sign your limited edition prints with your name, an image number and date. In all cases it must include the quantity of the edition and the number in sequence of the print your are signing.

Again:

WILLIAM R. EASTMAN III
1001 Nov. 74 1/50

In the majority of cases the lower number prints (1/50, 2/50, 3/50, etc.) will be more valuable than the higher number prints (47/50, 48/50, 49/50). In the case of woodcuts and lithographs, the earlier prints are of a greater quality than the later numbers. The reason for this is that the edges of the original becomes worn as more and more prints are pulled from it. Fine detail and color often tend to blur and mellow in the later prints. Traditionally, therefore, the earlier prints are more valuable. In the case of photography, there should be no difference at all between the first print and the last in an edition, unless, of course, the photographer stays up all night printing and gets sloppy near the end. Still, you will find that your lower numbered prints will be more valuable. For this reason it might be worth while to hold back a few early numbers for your best customers or for a better price as the edition becomes sold out.

If you also sign on the print itself, leave out the date and try to sign on a single line, generally in an inconspicuous place. You want people to enjoy your print, not your signature.

MATTING AND FRAMING YOUR WORK

As I mentioned earlier, all the work you offer for sale should be matted. Matting forms the foundation for your print; it gives a feeling of permanence and adds professionalism to your work. Most important, proper matting can dramatically enhance your print and increase its potential for sale.

Many artists and photographers purposely pick up subtle colors from within their prints and emphasize these colors by using mats of a similar or contrasting color. Enhancing prints through the use of colored mats calls for strong personal judgment and often a certain amount of good taste. There are many photographers and artists who are exceptionally skilled at what they do, but who absolutely cannot color-coordinate their prints and mats. Beautiful artwork in garish mats and frames simply does not sell.

If you do decide to try different colored mats, seek out your local frame shop for advice. Visit all the galleries you can find and pay attention to what other successful artists have done. You don't have to copy but there's nothing wrong with imitating success by seeing what works for others. Print enhancement through matting and framing is a skill in itself, but one that can add profit and prestige to your work.

In the majority of cases you will probably decide to go with a simple white mat. It is the most versatile in that it can be hung virtually anywhere and usually it is less expensive. There are several styles available with different surfaces and costs. I don't have any set answers for you. This is a matter of personal taste and budget. Often I've found that a rough surface or one that is dimpled looks and feels more expensive. Go with class as long as it is in the budget.

A brief word about costs. We will discuss this in more depth in the section on marketing. Every wholesaler knows that a penny spent on the production level can increase retail prices by as much as five or ten cents. There are only two reasons you should spend a lot of money on matting and framing. The first is if you are offering a very exclusive edition of artwork. Limited Edition art sells for more and people expect to pay for the extra touches. The second reason for putting a lot into matting, framing, etc., is if you have a volume deal and you can buy the materials for a smaller unit cost.

A BALLPARK FIGURE ON WHAT IT WILL COST YOU

Take the size of your print. Let's say 16x20. Add two inches all around. Now it's 20x24. Add them together:

20
24
44 add decimal and extra 0. $4.40 is your cost.

This is the basic way a frame shop should figure his charge for materials and labor for matting a 16x20 with a two inch margin based on the average cost of a medium-priced mat board. If you have someone else mat your work he is probably charging too much. Naturally, if you do the work yourself, you can probably cut this in about half.

DRY MOUNTING

Dry mounting is the most common method of affixing a photographic print to mat board or other surfaces. Dry mounting tissue is heat sensitive and bonds to both the print and the backing surface. For permanent, professional prints you must use a dry mount press which allows the two surfaces to be bonded under evenly distributed heat and pressure. In the event that you are not already familiar with the skills and techniques involved in dry mounting, I suggest that you do a lot of practicing on black and white prints before you attempt mounting your best art work. Dry mounting is not difficult but it does require a certain amount of practice. Dry mounting resin-coated papers demands extra caution as these papers melt and buckle under excessive heat.

Dry mounting is generally an acceptable way of preparing your prints for presentation. If the corners of the mat later become damaged or the mat itself becomes stained, a future owner can trim it flush with your print and remat your print. Dry mounting is probably the most efficient for any kind of volume printing that requires a matted surface or a print to be bonded to any surface for sale.

HINGE MATTING

Hinge matting is the major alternative to dry mounting. It requires two mats (or one mat and a backing board). Let's say that you wish to mount a 16x20 print with a three inch margin. Both boards would need to be 22x26. The board used to back the print need not be of high quality. In fact, if the matted print is to be placed into a frame, the backing board can be something as inexpensive as chipboard.

To hinge mat, the main mat is trimmed from the inside, or cut out as a window slightly smaller than your print. The print can then be lightly taped with masking tape behind the window. Because the print will be sandwiched between the backing board and the front mat, it is only necessary to tape along the top of the print. The two mats can then be spot-glued together with rubber cement.

Hinge mounting is preferred in art circles. The reason is that it gives maximum protection to the print while allowing it to be rematted as necessary without damage to the print. Your very finest and most expensive prints should be backed on rag board.

Because of its cloth content it is less likely to discolor and stain the print in front of it.

DOUBLE MATTING

Double matting costs a little more but can be a very effective way to jazz up your prints. It is essentially a frame within a frame. The second mat is 'window cut' perhaps a half an inch or less larger than the inside mat. Both mats are of compatible, though contrasting, shades and each should accent colors within the photograph.

Any gallery should have plenty of examples of double matting. It is an excellent way to add another touch of class to your prints. Just keep in mind your added cost versus the return. If it helps sell *your* prints – do it!

SEAL IT

Once your photograph is mounted on matte board you are ready for the most important step: SEAL IT!

The object is to keep out air, dust, moisture and anything else that might threaten the life of your work. Since many people still do not put their prints under glass, sealing them after mounting will increase their chances of surviving the rigors of time.

There are a large number of art sprays on the market. They come in all types, from dulling or matte sprays to clear or gloss sprays. Look for quality here; ask about any tendencies they might have to discolor or yellow through exposure to heat or light. If you want to add a special touch to your print at the same time you protect it, you might choose one of the texture sprays available through some art dealers. These can be especially attractive and make your customer think he is getting something extra.

Work that is not sprayed has virtually no protection. Make sure you cover the entire print and spray the edges between print and matte as well.

TO FRAME OR NOT TO FRAME

There can be no question that framing your work will greatly increase its value and appeal. In fact there are times when not framing your work can be a detriment to its sale. If certain pieces of your work are scheduled to be hung in art galleries or exhibits

— you should definitely give a lot of thought to framing.

There are a multitude of materials available for frames. Among the most popular for photo art are wood and metal frames. If you are working in standard sizes, i.e., 16x20, 20x24, etc., you will find that many metal and wood frames are available pre-cut from many art and frame shops. These will range in price from around $10 for an aluminum frame kit to $25 for elaborate wooden frames. You can buy the materials yourself and build your own frames but chances are this will add even more dollars to the cost of framing.

One company out of Kansas City manufactures its own frames for much less than you can build your own. They also import finished frames from Mexico and Taiwan. I would suggest that you spring for postage to write to them for a free catalogue. Not only will you get an idea about costs and the wide range of frames available — but they have an excellent section in their catalogue on matting.

Write to: Picture Frames by Caroline Kingcade
1313 Atlantic Street
N. Kansas City, MO 64116

Cost remains the single drawback for framing the majority of your work. If your production costs start running more than $30 or $40 for printing, matting, and framing — then your prints are going to have to sell from between $50 and $100 to make it worth your while.

One suggestion I would make is to frame at least some of your work so that it is available at your studio or for shows, etc. I've found that carrying one fully framed and matted photograph along with my portable portfolio does increase sales. Buyers are able to get a better idea of just how good your work can really look and they start looking around the room for somewhere to hang it.

If patrons are interested in buying your work already framed, you can show them samples or assure them that you will be able to make the arrangements for them. It is important to break down the cost of your prints matted versus framed. People don't mind having to pay more to have your photos framed, but if the only price you give them is pre-framed, it may kill the sale because it is already out of their price range.

Many people will prefer to buy your work matted but without the frame. This will give them the opportunity to personalize your photos for their own living rooms and offices. Many interior designers and architects have their own arrangements for framing. They prefer to have their people finish all artwork so that it will fit into the settings they are working on at the time.

If your work is to appear in art shows, it need not be framed, but there is no doubt that it will receive more attention if it is. The more professional your work appears in public places, the quicker it will be recognized and desired. So let your best face show. Almost certainly, if your work is to be hung in a fine gallery, it should be framed. Additional, unframed prints can always be made available behind the counter. Both prices should appear on the work that is hanging.

HOW LARGE SHOULD YOUR PRINTS BE?

If your work is to be sold as a limited edition or as art intended for commercial use (i.e.: to decorate offices, public places, etc.), your prints should not be less than 16x20 in size. Work that is meant for display needs to be large enough to be seen and appreciated from ten to twenty feet away. Also, work 16x20 and larger is easier and more realistic to sell. People are used to buying framed artwork up to poster size for reasonable amounts of money. Anything under 16x20 will not dominate a wall or accent office space.

When I first started out, I made the mistake of trying to sell 11x14 prints. By the time I had them printed, matted and sprayed, my cost was running from $25 to $30. I tried selling them between $45 and $60 but they just didn't move. People raved about the photos, but $15 to $20 seemed to be about the top price many of them wanted to pay. When I increased the size of the prints to 16x20, sales increased four hundred per cent simply because people felt they were starting to pay for what they were getting.

This does not mean that smaller prints will not sell. On the contrary. One local photographer here in Colorado has set up a consignment system with several small mall shops. He supplies mounted prints from 5x7 to 16x20 of about thirty different images. These are mass produced and unlimited. Customers can buy the same image in any of four sizes: 5x7, 8x10, 11x14, 16x20. Naturally, the prices vary. The thing that makes it work is that all of these prints were printed and packaged ahead of time in volume. Each mounted print is signed and wrapped in clear plastic.

Because his volume cost per unit is so small, he can sell these prints from between $3.50 and $5.00 for the 5x7's to $25 for the unframed 16x20's. This price may still seem somewhat high to the normal consumer, but it is realistic and they feel they are buying something special, something of value. Even teenagers can scrape up the money to buy this kind of personalized art. Volume sales in high traffic areas make it work.

Incidentally, one shop does display some of his larger prints in frames. Frames are available for all sizes separately. Breaking the cost down in this way gives people the chance to buy just what they need. The same shop also carries several of the photographer's limited edition prints. These are framed and expensive – between $75 and $250 depending on size, number in edition and frames available.

From a marketing standpoint, this particular arrangement is fantastic! There is work available in all price ranges: this allows the low priced, volume work to absorb much of the high overhead that goes hand in hand with limited editions. An inexpensive, black and white brochure is available on the artist, his background, credits, and some of his work. The fact that inexpensive prints are available to anyone actually increases the photographer's popularity and the potential for limited edition sales. In fact, the small prints are some of the best publicity the photographer can have. They circulate his name and skill while they create a desire for his more expensive images.

Although this particular technique has been very successful for one photographer, it does not automatically mean that it is for you. One thing I continue to stress every few paragraphs is cost and investment versus return. A setup such as this requires a good amount of capital up front. If the project flops you are going to be stuck with virtually hundreds of prints. Once you have sold your work to commercial outlets (designers, banks, industries, etc.) then is the time to consider putting out a retail selection for the public. Always start out small and test, test, test. Only after you have some definite statistics that YOUR work is salable and that YOUR project is feasible, should you run down to the bank to borrow money for your print business.

QUANTITY IN A LIMITED EDITION

These days limited editions are being sold in everything from cars, silver, jewelry, pottery, porcelain, bronzes, watercolors, lithographs, photographic prints, and more. Quantities of any particular edition may run from 25 to 5,000 – perhaps even more. It depends on the item and the muscle behind the marketing organization.

But how large should your selection of limited edition photographs be? The right answer to this question can easily mean the difference between your success or failure.

If you are going to market your edition nationally through a magazine or a chain store, chances are that you can go with a larger edition. For one thing, the advertising is going to be expensive. In order to break even or turn a profit you will either have to charge higher prices or have a larger edition to help average out the cost.

At most, you should not sell your work in an edition over 500. My personal feeling is that 300 should be tops for a national campaign. It is possible that a large chain store might want your signed and limited work. If they are big enough they might want a larger edition. If they were to buy several hundred to a thousand prints outright, you could probably get your unit cost printed and matted to under $10 for a 16x20. They, in turn, could frame it for another dollar or two and sell it for $35 to $40. A signed original by you for less than $40 – not bad, huh?

Chances are, unfortunately, that those original prints would never be worth much more than $40 to $60. There are simply too many of them and they would be too readily available for anyone who wanted to collect them. For your work to become valuable there has to be a serious shortage of supply versus demand.

Picasso seemed to learn this lesson very well. Later in life, his editions were only 50, and he was an artist of world acclaim. These prints were naturally snapped up immediately and were taken out of circulation. This is where the supply/demand psychology really begins to work for the artist. The public knows that if they don't buy your prints as soon as they are available, it will cost them twice the price when they do have a chance to buy. When this happens, speculators will start buying. These people couldn't care if they are buying pet rocks or brown paper bags, as long as there is a chance they will increase in value.

Chances are very good that your work will not become as popular as Picasso's or Ansel Adams', at least not in the foreseeable future.

The fact is, however, that smaller editions are the best way to go. The sooner an edition sells out, the quicker it will begin to appreciate in value. Once you have two or three images sold out, people will begin to pay serious attention to your work. The buying motive of: "Oh, I can get one of those next month when my taxes come in", or "Gee, I bet my wife would enjoy that for her birthday in August", will become "Boy, I'd better pick that up now while it is still available".

A second reason for a smaller edition is price. If people have to pay $75 to $300 for an edition of 300, they may become very reluctant to buy. If they have to pay the same amount for an edition of 50 the price becomes more realistic and they feel that they are getting their money's worth.

To start out then, I suggest that you keep your limited edition prints in quantities of 25 to 50. This will greatly increase their chance of selling and your chance for success. Price for a 16x20, for example, should range from $75 to $250 depending on the quality and content of your work, your popularity as a photographer, and the demand for your images.

PROTECTING YOUR WORK

One of the biggest headaches concerning photographic art is the potential for illegal copies, forgeries and fakes. This is where the real nightmares begin for not only the dealer and buyer but for the artist or photographer who created the image.

As I mentioned earlier, all of your work is covered under common law copyright. The problem lies not so much with the legal question of someone copying your work as much as with catching them doing it.

This is especially a problem with limited edition prints. When someone buys one of your original works of art, they are entitled to a little extra protection for their investment. Earlier we looked at the practice of signing your prints both on the matte and the photograph. Forgery or illegal copies are one of the strongest reasons for signing your print on the photograph itself. One of the most unfortunate problems concerning photographic art is that it can be easily and professionally copied via photography. An unsigned print could be reproduced perfectly without detection, distributed through perfectly legitimate channels and sold without your permission and often without your knowledge. The destructive part of this is that it will absolutely ruin the future value of your work. By signing the print directly on the photograph, you give yourself some small protection against forgers. If the photograph is now copied, the signature will come out in photographic silver, rather than india ink, blood — or whatever else you signed it with.

Signing the print on the photograph will give you some protection against forgeries, but it is by no means a foolproof system. One method I have discovered for protecting prints is a notarized authorization sheet. Your first responsibility once you decide to release any of your photographic art, is to set up a permanent recording system. This need be nothing more than a hardbound notebook where you can keep a running record of how many prints have been sold, to whom, for what price, how many were in the edition, what marketing method you used, etc.

Each print in a limited edition must be recorded. No, there isn't any law to this effect, it is simply good business — a necessity for you and your customer. If possible you should record each sale alongside the number of the print in the edition. This should include the buyer's name and address. There are any number of reasons that this is a good policy. To begin with, you now have the name and address of someone who owns one of your prints. Your easiest sales come from people who already made the buying decision once. If they own one of your limited editions, chances are they will be interested in seeing new editions as they become available.

A second reason for recording names and addresses is in the event someone contacts you about one of your prints that is sold out. You now have names and addresses where he might be able to purchase one of your prints. Now, you have pleased both parties, the one who just sold one of your prints for a profit, and the new investor who will be eager to consider your next image.

Personally, I like to take the recording system one step further. In my case I use an attorney, although a public accountant or notary public will do as well. When I prepare a list of a new edition, I make two copies, one for me and one for my attorney, each of which can be kept current as prints are sold and re-sold.

Next I prepare the authorization sheet which contains the following items:

1. The name of the print and its image number. This is generally centered at the top as a title.
2. A description of the photograph. Possibly even a poem to set the mood. The idea is to personalize everything as much as possible.

3. The number in the edition followed by the print sequence number and the present date.
4. Beneath this my signature.
5. Below this leave room for the buyer's name and address.

Note: Numbers 3, 4, and 5 should be placed on the left side of the page. On the right hand side of the page leave room for:

6. The notary public's seal, signature and date. (Note: Each state seems to require their notary public to use a slightly different statement along with their seal and signature: "So and so, appearing before me, etc." Check with your local notary. He will know how to do it. A good idea is to check with your bank. Most of them will provide you with free notary service if you are a good customer.

This is the authorization sheet for my image "The Flying Dutchman":

THE FLYING DUTCHMAN
#1001

When I think of the sea, I think of brine and salt air, of velvet evenings and unpredictable winds. I think of ruddy-faced men battling the elements – tempest, tides and desert islands.

Mysterious always, the sea is a place where fables and legends are spawned, be they tales of white whales or pirates and lost treasure. But to me, one of the most fascinating romances surrounding the sea has been the world of sailing ships and the legend of the Flying Dutchman.

My own version of the Flying Dutchman is a combination of two images.

The first was a frontal shot of the four-masted schooner, Fantome, taken in the Bahamas from a motor launch. Exposure on Kodachrome 25 was 1/250th of a second at f/8.

The second shot was taken on my return to Dallas, over the Gulf of Mexico. I had been asleep and the sun, shining directly on my face woke me in time to see that vast ocean of ruffled clouds suspended some twenty thousand feet over the blue gulf waters. The idea immediately crystallized and I shot over six rolls of film in the next few minutes in order to get just the right shot to combine with the Fantome photo. Exposure was 1/500 at f/11 on Kodachrome 25.

The final image was combined on a Honeywell Repronar on Ektachrome X at an exposure of 23 flashes on High at f/22.

Limited Edition of 300
Print No. 1/300
March 17, 1975

This print was purchased by:

____

____

____

On this 17th day of March, 1978, appeared before me, William R. Eastman III to sign his name and verify that Image 1001, print 1/300 has been set aside for ____________ ________________.

____

NOTARY PUBLIC

A separate authorization sheet should be printed for each print in your edition. It should be signed and notarized either when the entire edition is printed, or one at a time prior to the sale.

An authorization sheet such as this is your customer's best protection against your making illegal prints, against forgers, thieves and anyone else who might duplicate your prints. Because of your preparation and record keeping, these people can now verify the sale of each print in the edition: you, your accountant or attorney, and the final customer. If a print is later sold or bought at an auction, the authorization sheet will help guarantee its authenticity.

SECTION III
MARKETING YOUR PRINTS

PRICING

One of the most difficult problems with selling photography in any form is pricing. Pricing seems to be closely linked with the black arts. Professional photographers, art directors and various photo agencies always manage to come up with a dozen different prices for the same piece of photographic work. A New York Ad Agency will likely bill $200 for the same photography a local Utah photographer will charge out at $20. The rule of thumb seems to be what the market will bear. Unfortunately, professionals often overprice their work (which makes the market bad) and amateurs tend to underprice (which destroys the market).

So let's try and be realistic as well as flexible. Certainly, geographic location will have some effect on both the market for your prints as well as the price you can expect. The quality of your work will increase or decrease its value — and the price you can get. Content, framing, extra frills, etc., will naturally affect the price. If you are in an area where wildlife art sells well you can probably get more for your prints than you could in an area where no one is interested in wildlife.

Finally, who you are and your reputation in the field will greatly influence the price you can expect from your work. We will discuss this in more depth in the next section on credibility. Keeping all of these things in mind, let's try to come up with a formula that will help you set a fair and reasonable price for your photographic art.

The first step is to look at the actual physical cost to you of your photographic print. Except in the very rare case you should not include any costs relating to the actual taking of the picture. Remember, art prints are a supplemental income off your photography. If you spend thousands of dollars going to Africa on a photo safari don't expect to add the price of your trip onto your limited edition or other art prints. On the other hand, your print sales will definitely help absorb a lot of expenses.

Basically your expenses will include any of the following:

1. PREPARATION: Internegs, retouching, any other art work related to preparing your negative or transparency for printing.
2. PRINT COST: If you work through a lab, the cost of printing, spotting, etc. Anything related to the cost to you per print. If you do your own printing, you know how to average out everything and come up with a realistic cost.
3. MATTING: Any costs relating to materials and labor for matting and sealing of your print.
4. FRAMING: Same as above, if applicable.
5. SPECIAL FEATURES: If you are producing a limited edition this would include your printing costs for authorization sheets, brochures, notary fees, etc.

All costs which are one time expenses, i.e., internegatives, authorization sheets, etc., should be averaged out over the total number of prints you plan on making. Once you have arrived at the cost per print you can begin to figure the price a print should sell for under different conditions.

Let's say that you are going to produce a 16x20 print. As you are working from a slide, you will need an interneg. These prints must be spotted and mounted on 20x24 matte board. There will be an additional charge to have a spray texture applied.

Cost for one 16x20 print:	$18.50	(Price decreases with volume)
Interneg: ($5.00)	.10	(Average over 50 prints)
Mounting:	3.50	(Fixed price)
Spotting:	1.50	
Spray:	.85	
	$24.45	
Authorization Sheets		
Notary:	1.50	(Per sheet)
Printing costs:	.30	(Per sheet)
	$ 1.80	
Framing:	$19.50	

The cost we have established is for one print. Depending on whether or not you do your own printing, matting, and framing, and depending on the quality of the prints (most good commercial labs offer several grades of prints), this price is about average. It is possible that the print we have listed at $24.45 could cost you anywhere from about $11.00 to $75.00.

If you are producing a limited edition, your base cost per print is now $24.45 plus $1.80 plus $19.50. Or $26.25 unframed and $45.75 framed.

Before we go further let's note that if you make more than one print at a time, you can dramatically reduce this cost.

Cost for one 16x20 print	$18.50 per print
Cost for ten $109.49	$10.90 per print
Cost for twenty-five $196.64	$ 7.86 per print
Cost for fifty $327.89	$ 6.55 per print

Even if we figure that your other costs are fixed, this will decrease the individual cost per print for one from $24.45 to $12.50 for 50 prints.

As a rule of thumb, your mark-up will range from 50% to 300% — *depending on the circumstances.*

UNLIMITED PRINTS SOLD THROUGH DEALERS ON CONSIGNMENT

A great number of art dealers, gift shops and other art-oriented outlets will accept your work on consignment only. If you are a beginner, consignment is definitely worth considering. It will give you a lot of exposure and make it easier for you to sell your work direct later on. If a dealer finds that your work does sell, chances are he may decide that he'd rather buy your work outright and make a better profit on it.

The advantage of consignment is that most dealers will gladly accept your work if it is at all good. The exposure is well worth it to you.

The disadvantage is that you will have a lot of prints out that will not sell immediately. It will probably cost you several hundred dollars up front to get your work prepared and out, and in the end you may sell only a small percentage of these prints. (The advertising value is still worth considering, especially if you have other outlets for your work.)

A dealer will probably want anywhere from twenty to fifty per cent of the retail price of the work. Once he gets paid, you collect.

The maximum the market will bear on a signed, matted, unlimited, unframed print is probably about $65 (16x20). The best retail price if you wish to sell more than an occasional print would probably range between $35 and $45.

If your cost on the print is $24.50, a hundred per cent mark-up is $49. If the dealer takes thirty percent ($14.70) then you only make $19.85. If you reduce the price to fit into the $35 to $45 range you are going to get a lot of exposure but not much profit.

It's obvious that the only way to work on consignment is to print in volume and cut your costs as much as possible.

Framing may also help you get a little better price for your prints. I would suggest that you discuss the possibility of splitting framing costs with individual dealers. Sometimes this works and it can be a great help. Remember, anything you can do to encourage a dealer to invest even a small amount in your work will help motivate him to push your prints and make sales for you. Framed prints will probably sell for $35 to $45 more.

If your work is exceptionally good it will command higher prices. The only way to know for certain what your particular market will bear is to constantly test both markets and prices.

Printing in volume, whether you are selling direct or on consignment, will still get your work to the retail level at a smaller price. It will require a larger investment and more risk. You will have to decide for yourself whether it is worth it.

DIRECT DEALER SALES

Selling direct to a dealer may be difficult but it is still the best way to go when you can do it. Because your risk is less, your profits need not be as high. Once the ball gets rolling you can start printing in volume and really begin making headway.

Unless it is an exclusive shop, I would suggest no more than a fifty to one hundred per cent mark-up. You will be getting a fair price for your prints and the dealer will be able to be more flexible with cost.

Unless you have a very good deal going on your framing, I would also suggest that you offer your prints matted but not framed. Most dealers have their own framing people. If you allow them to control this angle of cost they will be able to save more money. Yes, of course, that's something that you could have made a few more pennies on, but if it helps the dealer sell more of your prints, then you are better off in the long run. Be flexible and try to cooperate any way you can. It will strengthen your relationship with the dealer.

SELLING DIRECT

This may sound like door to door but it is the most effective way for you to make large print sales, a reasonable profit, and make your customer feel like he is getting something very special indeed. There is, of course, no middleman involved. You are the whole production and sales force.

The best rule here is a forty to eighty per cent mark-up over your single print cost. The same mark-up applies to framing, though you might want to use the lower half of the scale.

If a bank or industry wants more than just a few of your pictures, be competitive and give them the best deal you can. These are the best types of customers you can have: their word of mouth to other banks and corporate offices will guarantee you other customers. Those few extra dollars you shaved off what you were going to charge will more than pay for itself in new orders. Always be as fair and considerate as you can when you sell direct. Don't be afraid to break down your actual costs and discuss with your prospect what they feel would be a fair profit for you. They are businessmen and know the facts of life. They will respect you for being sincere and honest.

I recently had one of my old accounts call me from out of state. They weren't satisfied with the new local talent that was available and wanted to know if I would mind doing an assignment for them. I said sure. I quoted them my most fair price, adding at the same time that I should probably charge them another fifty per cent. The client insisted that I charge him the higher price. I had always been fair with him and this time he needed me to do a favor for him.

WHOLESALE PRICING

This is where you really have to sharpen your pencil and be competitive. If you are going to interest a wholesaler at all you are going to have to demonstrate to him that you have more than just talent.

Let's say that a print costs you $5.00 to produce. You in turn sell it to a wholesaler for $7.50. By the time he packs it and distributes it to the dealers around the country, his cost per print has risen to $11. He now sells it to the dealer for $16. The dealer in turn puts it into inventory and lists it for $29.95. These costs are approximate, but as you can see, it is not unreasonable that your print will sell from six to eight times what it cost you to produce.

If the wholesaler is interested in buying any of your work you should discuss the quantity he is interested in first. Be able to figure your exact cost on production. This should include any transportation or other incidental costs for that particular project. Use your volume per-print cost as your base. Start with a seventy-five per cent mark-up. If the wholesaler thinks this is too much, he will let you know. Drop to fifty per cent: this is where you should remain if at all possible. Absolutely do not go under twenty-five per cent. The only times you should consider these extremely low mark-ups is if you are talking a very large deal of a thousand prints or more.

Look at wholesaling as not how much you make per print but as how much you make per project. Figure your profit from your time and effort as well as the value of the prints you are selling.

PRICING YOUR LIMITED EDITIONS

Your limited edition prints are worth more. Not so much for their future value but because they are limited, beautiful, and unique.

To begin with figure your base cost for printing, matting, framing, etc. As before, always work with two prices, framed and unframed. Next, add fifty per cent as your advertising cost. Believe me, you will be lucky if your advertising and promotional costs come in this low. The combination of these two costs now become your base cost for limited editions.

In a normal edition of between 50 and 300 your prints should retail between one hundred and two hundred per cent over your base price. That 16x20 we printed a while back for $25 would therefore sell on a retail level for between $75 and $150, but very special prints or prints by well known artists may sell for even more.

If you are selling to a retail outlet your mark-up should run from fifty to one hundred per cent.

You should make every effort to see that your prints retail for about the same price whether you sell them direct to the customer or they are sold through a retail outlet. It is all right if an art dealer or other retail outlet asks more for your prints than suggested retail. But under no circumstances should you sell your photos direct for more than they are available in stores. Once the edition is completely sold out, the selling price of your prints will vary depending on the current supply versus demand.

Often the earlier prints in a limited edition series will sell for more. Occasionally, an artist will hold onto several of the early prints in a series. These prints can usually be sold at a later date for a greater profit.

As you become better known you will probably be able to get greater prices for your work. Keep in mind as well that you will probably also be able to afford to make more prints at a time and thus take advantage of volume costs. It may even be that as you become more popular you will be able to sell your work for less and make more.

CREDIBILITY – THE MASTER TOUCH

Credibility is absolutely your greatest asset.

People should buy your art because it appeals to them, because they have a desire to own and possess the image you have created. In the beginning this is almost exactly what happens. If people like your work, they will buy it for art's sake.

The big question is whether or not they will be willing to pay the kind of price you must receive from your work to make it financially feasible for you to continue producing it. The question most people ask is, "Who is he, what has he done, is this just a lucky shot or is the man steeped in talent?" As your work becomes more and more available, people's curiosity will become further aroused.

It is important that people know as many of your credits as possible. If you are a famous *Playboy* photographer, let the public know. Include it in your biography sheet. It is a very strong selling point for your work. Not only will it help the art dealer ("This is one of the best prints by Joel Cary – you know the Playboy photographer") but it will give the customer a feeling of pride that he owns your work.

The sooner you can establish yourself as a serious professional, the faster your work will be accepted. Who you are and what you have done will not only give you valuable leverage for free publicity and advertising, it will open doors to direct sales, dealer sales, wholesalers, and the rest.

Credibility — who you are and what you have done — is an asset just as valuable as your skill and talent. It makes you believable.

Not too many years ago, I was trying to break into some tough freelance markets. I knew that my work was good enough but it was doubtful that people like Hallmark or Kodak would take the time to bother with another 'unknown'. Places like these are swamped daily with thousands of unsolicited photographs — the majority junk — from all over the country. Most of these never even reach the man at the top — the one who can make the decision to buy a new photographer's work.

There I was with a desk, a typewriter and a camera. It occurred to me that he had no way to judge me at all except by what he had in front of him. For all he knew I could be one of the hottest upcoming photographers around — or a slob. So I took my time and designed some unique stationery — not facy, but solid, tasteful and interesting. I made sure my cover letter was letter perfect. The writing was direct and professional. I packaged a sample of my slides in plastic sheets — well labeled and Felix Unger tidy. Everything was then packaged professionally, down to a self-addressed return envelope and a check to cover more than return postage. I sent the whole thing Air Mail, Certified, Return Receipt Requested.

About a month later I received my package back along with a letter from 'the man'. He liked my work and was holding one of my slides for further consideration. Could he see more?

In the years that followed I have continued to make sales in this manner, even garner some special assignments. I always list my credits to let the people know that I am serious and a professional. Packaging helps, too; mostly it allows people to keep an open mind until they have read what you have to say or seen what you have to show them.

If you have a serious lack of credits, work on getting some. If your work is even mediocre it will still sell. When it comes to getting yourself published, persistance is often more important than talent.

If you don't have credits now, find something unique about your photography or your background that will be interesting to people. If you have a rather unique approach to your pictures, it's a selling point. People will probably be interested in knowing about it.

GETTING STARTED IN YOUR OWN BACKYARD

Once you have all the groundwork put together you are ready to get out and start selling. Although there are many different types of people and businesses you will be approaching, all of these can be put into two categories.

1. People who will sell your work for you.
2. People you will sell your work directly to.

In the first category we include architects, wholesalers, interior designers, art dealers, and all other retail outlets.

In the second are private sales, banks, industries, and any other commercial or private accounts that you might approach directly or through any form of advertising and publicity.

YOUR PORTFOLIO

Before you go out on the street you had better make sure your portfolio is in order.

You should have at least two images printed full size to show a customer exactly what they are buying. It will also give them a better idea of what it will look like on the wall. One of these prints should be framed, the other not. Image size should be at least 16x20 or 20x24. Make certain these prints are your very best images.

The next thing you will need is some way to show a large selection of your images, probably fifty to two hundred. This selection must show the full diversity of your work. The object is to have something for everyone.

Many photographers like to carry around a couple of trays of slides. This isn't a bad way to work because you can blow your pictures up and preview a lot of slides in a short time. Personally, I cringe at the very thought of putting any of my original slides in a projector – ever! Whether or not you decide to show originals or high quality dupes is up to you. Certainly this is a less expensive way to show your samples.

A second method is to prepare a large attractive scrapbook filled with prints that you have available for sale. These prints should be categorized according to subject, technique, etc. They should not be smaller than 4x5 or 5x7. There is no need to fill the book with 8x10's. Your large prints will give people the impact you need to generate sales.

It would also be helpful if you worked up a couple of price sheets. Put them on your stationery to make them look more professional. When you leave them behind it will help people identify you and make it easier for them to get in touch. You should have separate price sheets for the two categories above.

If you do not have a formal brochure, you should have a separate biography page attached to your price list. This will include any 'useful' information on your company, prints, background, credits, etc.

APPROACHING YOUR CLIENT

Anytime you are going to deal in person with a business or professional client, remember that you are a businessman just as he is. Whenever possible, you should call in advance for an appointment. Let him or his secretary know who you are and what you wish to discuss. You may find it to your advantage to make one or more preliminary calls to the company headquarters for the purpose of finding out whom to contact and what kind of work they have purchased in the past.

ABSOLUTELY DO NOT SELL ON THE TELEPHONE!

Once you have your man on the line (or his secretary) the tendency is to start building enthusiasm about your product. Don't do it! Don't give them the opportunity to prejudge you or your ideas before they have seen your work.

If he tries to turn you off, let him know that you have something special, but don't go into extensive details. Ask for an appointment – even just a few minutes. Even if you don't make a sale to the company you will still have made an important contact who might be able to steer you somewhere else. Even if someone is impressed with your work and your ideas it does not follow that he will automatically buy your prints on the spot.

The biggest advantage of an appointment is that you will have an opportunity to spend at least a few private moments with your client. He will have time to look at your work and consider its potential for him or his company. Without an appointment you will probably be interrupted constantly. Your product and your pitch will never get off the ground.

If you must call 'cold', ask to see your contact for just a brief moment. If you succeed, show and then tell. Get his curiosity aroused before you let him know your life story. If at all possible, ask him if there would be a more convenient time when you can come back and have a few minutes with him.

The greatest thing I've learned about selling is to take your time. The longer you are able to keep another person's interest in what you are telling him, the better chance you have of closing a sale.

THE ARCHITECT AND INTERIOR DESIGNER

Both of these people have something very valuable in common: they have established clients who are used to spending money to decorate homes, offices and buildings.

Most of them are interested in talking with new talent. This is especially true if you have a new concept available that will help them sell their other products and services. Remember, designers generally work on commission and they are very competitive. If you give them something they can sell to give them an edge on their market, they will love you for it.

This brings up an important point. Interior designers, architects, and artists (of all kinds) have long walked hand in hand. It is important for you to get into the partnership spirit. You have something that can help the other.

It is very possible that many interior designers are not yet familiar with the full applications of photographic art. It is just as important for you to sell and educate them to the concept as it is to sell your own work.

There are many ways you can work together with interior designers. Sharing customers is one. You will be on the road looking for industrial accounts for your prints. These people are often looking for the services of a good designer. Let a potential designer or architect know that you will spread the word about his business. If you own a studio, offer to share some of these customers with him on future projects.

Something that can work out exceptionally well is an educational program you and the designer set up together. You hold a free seminar for certain business owners and members of the public: send out invitations to a seminar on decorating with photographic art in the home and office. Show slides and both of you give a lecture on what each of you knows best. By spending time to educate the public in this way both of you will land clients.

You might consider contacting the regional chapter of the American Society of Interior Designers and request a list of members in your area. Remember, educating them is just as important as selling them your work.

I suggest you contact:

Eastman Kodak Company
Dept. 454
343 State Street
Rochester, New York 14650

Ask them to send you a copy of their booklet, "Decorating with Photographic Art". It contains many good color illustrations of rooms decorated with photography. This also can be a useful tool when you approach any of your clients, especially designers.

One last thing: don't forget to point out to designers and architects that photographic art is a natural for industrial buildings. As we mentioned earlier, there is nothing a business or industry likes better than quality photography on the walls showing its business in action. It gives cohesiveness and a sense of goal achievement to fellow workers. It can also do a lot to establish a strong public image for visitors.

ART DEALERS AND GIFT SHOPS

Approach by appointment whenever possible.

The biggest obstacle here is how you answer the question: "Will your photographic art sell?" Art Dealers make their bread and butter from selling art. Unlike the designer who has other products and services to sell, the Art Dealer has a limited amount of inventory he can display. If the work doesn't sell, he is out of business.

Getting in the door on consignment will probably not be that difficult. The less risk the dealer has to assume, the better your chances are that he will carry some of your work. By the same token, the less he is involved, the less he will be inclined to push your work.

If you are going to get in the door and see money up front, you will need every tool you can carry. This means a lot of credibility and strong presentation on the various ways photography can be used in home and office decoration. You are going to have to convince the dealer that photography is being accepted as art, that it will sell, that art buyers will collect it as an investment.

One thing that will help immeasurably is solid proof that other people in the same area are buying your photography for their homes and offices. This is where your all-'round sales program will benefit you. If you have sold a set of prints to a local bank or corporate office, make sure the dealer knows about it. If several prominent people have purchased your prints for their homes, let him know. The sooner you can establish a demand for your work, the quicker an art dealer will dip into his pocket for a checkbook. Remember, keep your prices competitive. You have to help him make a profit if you want him to support you. If necessary, sit down with the dealer and discuss the price range of his clientele. Try to work out projects and prints that will fit into this range.

In fact, any time you can sit down with a dealer and discuss his industry – what is selling, who is buying, and for how much – do it! The more inside knowledge you can accumulate on the art market, the bigger the edge you will have when it comes to selling your work.

SELLING DIRECT TO THE CONSUMER

Approaching banks and other local businesses is a fairly simple matter. When possible, get in the door with an appointment. The kind of businesses to look for are any types of professional offices or areas where the public must wait or linger. These would include law, doctors', or accountants' offices, travel agencies, restaurants, real estate offices and hundreds of others. Your best list here is the yellow pages.

The best way to approach these kind of businesses is not for individual print sales. Instead, work up several different types of package deals. Two prints, six prints, ten prints, etc. A selection of four or five different prints in a package; a nature package; a pop art package; a sports package. The combinations are endless.

Package deals give you a lot of flexibility as well. They give you a chance to sell several prints at the same time and thus not only increase your profit, but give you the option of modifying your prices to fit the budget. If you find a client who really likes your work, but can't afford it even at your package price (or needs a little additional motivation), you can modify a package on the spot to meet his or her needs.

Remember, know your costs exactly. If you have to spend an hour memorizing them, do it. You must be able to accurately bid a job on the spot. If you can't close a deal on the first meeting, always keep trying. You will make more and better sales, however, if you can get a positive commitment on the first meeting. For this you need to be prepared.

It also doesn't hurt to do a little ground work before you walk into a bank or a new restaurant. Learn as much about the business and the tastes of the personalities that head it as you can. If you can walk in the door with fresh ideas made to order, it will guarantee you sales.

INDUSTRIES: TELLING THE CORPORATE STORY

Selling the corporate story to industries is a challenge with very profitable possibilities. Not only are you charging for your photographic prints, but also for your time and photography.

More and more industries and large corporations are turning on their lobbies and offices with photographs distinguishing different aspects of their business. The idea is easy to sell, and it will give you excellent exposure, too.

You should approach these people the same way you reach banks and other businesses. The first objective — as always — is to sell them on your photography. Once you have succeeded in this you can bring up the option of photographing their businesses from the inside out.

If you cannot sell them on the corporate approach, the odds are still good that you can interest them in one of your other standard packages.

THE PUBLIC AT HOME

Don't try it. Entering your work in art shows or church exhibits, mall exhibits, etc., is a good idea, especially if you can attend to talk to people about your work and hand out some type of sales materials. But, never door to door. You will, from time to time, be invited into people's homes for private showings. Put on your best show, but don't pitch. Don't talk about price unless you are asked. Show your work, give any background that you think might be of interest and leave it at that. People know you are in business, so let them pop the question. If they drop their jaws at the prices, don't let it disturb you. Above all, don't do anything to make them think you feel they aren't good enough for your work. If you are showing them limited editions, explain that they are limited, that's why the price is so much more. Then show some of your other work. Suggest that they might be interested in some of your unlimited artwork. Be flexible.

YOU CAN GET FREE ADVERTISING AND PUBLICITY

The rarest coin on earth wouldn't be worth a penny to you unless: a) someone knew you owned it, and b) they learned that it was for sale. The same applies to photography. Unless people know that you have a product and that it is for sale, you will have no customers.

We have discussed various ways to market your photographs directly to potential buyers. But these people are only a portion of the pie. To reach the rest of the world, we need to look at the often expensive area of advertising and publicity.

Exposure is the key to the success of any product, while undercapitalization, lack of experience or poor money management are the causes of failure for most businesses.

Those sales you make directly will actually give you a large amount of free exposure. Dealers who carry your work will discuss it with other dealers. Banks, industries, and other businesses to whom you have sold your work will be in contact with fellow professionals. This 'word of mouth' advertising will generate new clients and sales for your product.

Finding other ways to spread the word about your work without cutting into your profits (or forcing you to raise prices) is a challenging necessity.

PUBLICITY

Publicity is generally considered to be non-sales-oriented exposure.

In an ad you set up its readers for a sale. This is done by:

1. Informing them of the existence of your product.
2. Creating a desire in them to own your product.
3. Asking them to buy your product.

Publicity, on the other hand, most often only fulfills the first two of these goals. Mainly, it focuses on the product itself.

"Sneaky Pete, working in his dungeon darkroom, has produced a unique new form of photographic art . . ."

If the publicity is interesting and informative, and gives a positive opinion or play to your product, then chances are favorable that this publicity will also create a desire for people to own your product. Once people have gotten this far they will generally want to know more about the product and where it is available. Good publicity will also include enough of the third step to direct these interested parties to where they can get more information on the product or service.

One of the most successful forms of free publicity I have received was from Meisel Photochrome, the lab where I do the majority of my work. They produce a color newsletter (or house organ) for all of their clients. It includes articles on techniques used by some of their clients, new products and services through the lab, and other items.

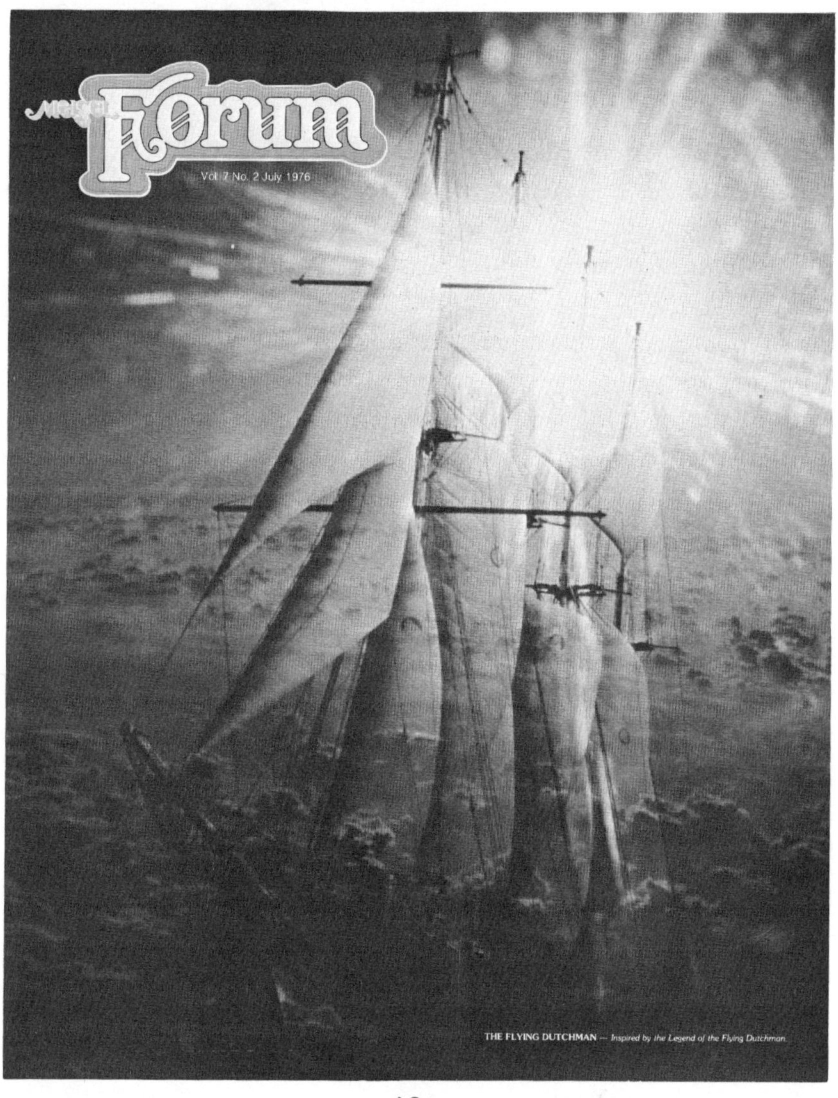

I sent the editor of the Meisel Forum some samples of my work along with a detailed description of how they were produced through his lab and marketed on the outside. He wrote back that he was very interested in the material and the approach. I sent him the additional information that he requested along with an address where interested parties could write for more information.

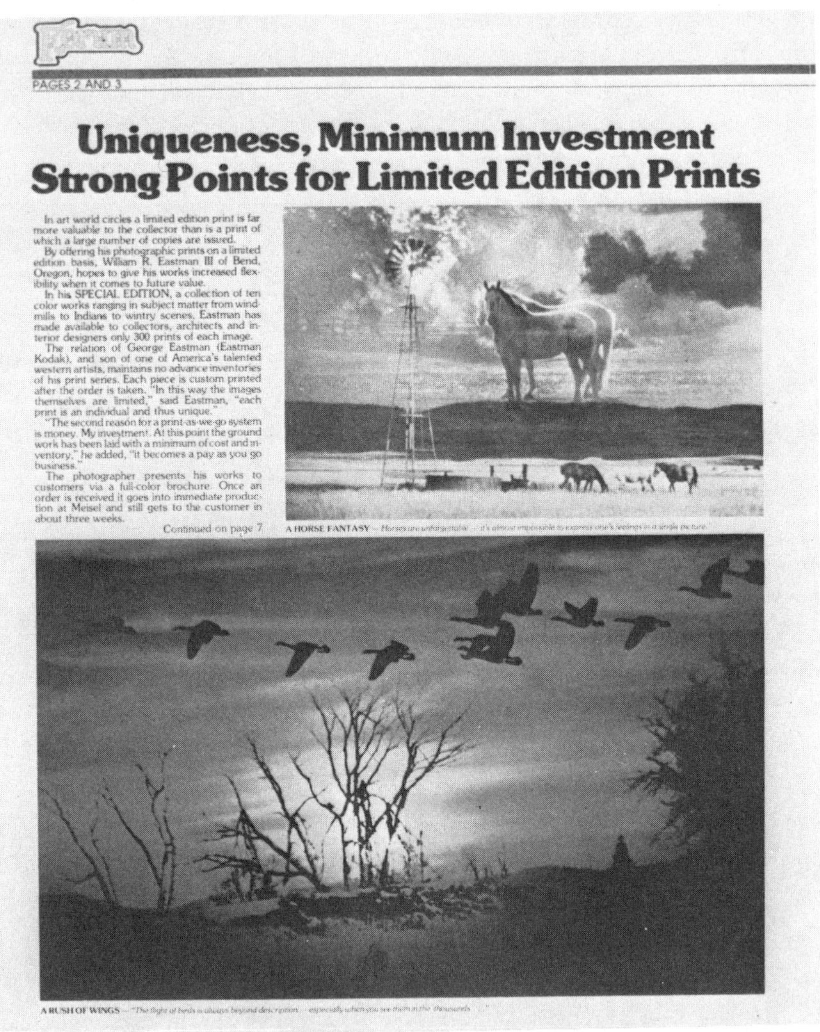

PAGES 2 AND 3

Uniqueness, Minimum Investment Strong Points for Limited Edition Prints

In art world circles a limited edition print is far more valuable to the collector than is a print of which a large number of copies are issued.

By offering his photographic prints on a limited edition basis, William R. Eastman III of Bend, Oregon, hopes to give his works increased flexibility when it comes to future value.

In his SPECIAL EDITION, a collection of ten color works ranging in subject matter from windmills to Indians to wintry scenes, Eastman has made available to collectors, architects and interior designers only 300 prints of each image.

The relation of George Eastman (Eastman Kodak), and son of one of America's talented western artists, maintains no advance inventories of his print series. Each piece is custom printed after the order is taken. "In this way the images themselves are limited," said Eastman, "each print is an individual and thus unique."

"The second reason for a print-as-we-go system is money. My investment. At this point the ground work has been laid with a minimum of cost and inventory," he added, "it becomes a pay as you go business."

The photographer presents his works to customers via a full-color brochure. Once an order is received it goes into immediate production at Meisel and still gets to the customer in about three weeks.

Continued on page 7

A HORSE FANTASY — *Horses are unforgettable — it's almost impossible to express one's feelings in a single picture.*

A RUSH OF WINGS — *"The flight of birds is always beyond description — especially when you see them in the thousands . . ."*

Several months later I received a Meisel Forum with my Flying Dutchman on the cover in full color. Inside were two more prints along with a larger banner headline: "Uniqueness, Minimum Investment: Strong Points for Limited Edition Prints." The article went on to explain who I was and what I was doing. At the end of the article was the address where photographers could write for a brochure and more information.

Not only did I receive excellent exposure from this article, I received a great deal of credibility. My name and my work were put into the public eye.

This kind of publicity is not as hard to get as it might seem. There are virtually hundreds of photo-oriented outlets that are looking for interesting material and dramatic photos for their readers. This list includes the major photo magazines, house organs (published by most of the major labs, trade magazines, and photo newsletters) and many local as well as national newspapers and magazines.

If you are a local photographer, it should be very simple to get in touch with the art editor of your home town newspaper. Local newspapers are always hungry for this kind of story: "Local photographer shows that photographic art has come of age!"; "Local photographer opens photographic art exhibit." There are dozens of angles. If you are entering your work in a regional show, work up a brief press release and take it down personally to the paper. If you win or place well, send them another press release to that effect. It is just as important to sell yourself as a photographer as it is to sell your work. This has nothing to do with ego or vanity – it has to do with business. People are not buying a product to wax their floors, they are buying a work of art for their pleasure and enjoyment. If names weren't important when it comes to buying for pleasure or status, then liquor merchants could bottle their champagne as 'good champagne' or 'cheap champagne'.

Once you have finished with the local papers, take a shot at the larger metropolitan papers. Many of these have Sunday supplements which feature local artists.

If you are especially astute at finding art in industrial photography, contact the editors of the thousands of industrial house organs. For lists of these you can check issues of Writer's Market, a massive book published by Writer's Digest. This includes just about every publication put out. Remember, house organs are sent to special interest parties. They are well read. If you can find a way to orient your photography or your approach to those specific groups, you will have little problem getting free exposure for your photographic prints.

Another set of publications are the fraternal magazines – Elks, Moose, VFW, etc. Work up an angle and give it a shot. The more exposure you get, the quicker your art print business is going to go into the black.

As you can see, the potentials for free publicity are endless. But let's go one step further.

What about the national magazines: Peterson's PhotoGraphic, Popular and Modern Photography, Camera 35? Several years ago I approached the editor of Camera 35 with an article idea on limited edition photographs. He was interested enough to request me to write an article and supply photos. At the last minute the whole project was turned down by the editorial staff because they thought it was too specialized. That may have been the case then, but it certainly is not now.

What about Money, Newsweek, Time, People – all of those massive exposure magazines? To the photographer with the right angle at the right time, all of these markets can be sold.

Women photographers can approach magazines like Ms., Ladies' Home Journal, etc. All of these magazines are looking for newsworthy items to pass along to their readers. If you can generate exposure on the local and regional levels, you can probably get your work displayed in larger, more formidable publications.

How do you approach these people?

It just isn't that difficult. The same photos and information you have produced for your direct sales will give you the angle you need to find free publicity. First, the photography must be unique, dramatic and exciting. Second, you must have a background that is interesting or unique. In short, you must have an angle that would be of national interest and as such, newsworthy. It may have something to do with your approach to photography, your marketing technique, or your work itself. All or some of these elements are present in anyone who becomes involved enough in photography to consider selling his work as art.

Step back and take a look at yourself and your work. What makes you tick? What makes your work appeal to other people? Go ahead – ask them. Find that particular angle that is most newsworthy. Then get going and motivate yourself and other people. Go out and get yourself the kind of publicity you deserve.

ADVERTISING

There simply isn't any such thing as free advertising. If it were free we wouldn't call it advertising – we would call it publicity or some other form of promotion. If it is advertising it is going to cost you something.

The game plan here is to find the best way to reach the public and get your sale for the smallest possible cost per sale! Believe it or not, there are a variety of ways to get advertising at a minimal cost – or risk – to you.

One of the most effective of these is trade-out advertising, referred to in the old days as barter. Your photographic prints are a product. As such they have a dollar value just like any other product. Using a barter or trade-out system, it is possible to get almost anything in return for your art prints, from accounting and legal services to advertising and other hard goods. All advertising outlets, newspapers, radio, magazines, or TV can be purchased with trade-out advertising. Over the past several years, I have personally arranged trade-outs in excess of several hundred thousand dollars for other major companies. The age of barter is not dead: it does require, however, a personal visit and a good sales pitch to pull off.

There are two major angles to use when you approach the media to trade for advertising. The first is for them to use your product themselves, as a bonus to salesmen or other employees, to hang on their office walls or waiting rooms, or to use as premiums or gifts for their other advertisers. If they have a client, for example, who spends $10,000 a year with their paper or station, then one of your prints might be a nice gift at the appropriate moment.

The second angle is to use your photo prints as prizes or premiums in promotions. A newspaper could use your prints as prizes in one of their subscription drives. A radio station or TV station might use them in one of their contests.

There are an incredible number of ways your photography can be used to the advantage of other businesses and publications. Talk to some local media owners and you will begin to see some of the angles.

Another low cost method of advertising is PI or PO ('per inquiry' or 'per order') advertising. The types of media who use this type of promotion most are radio and TV. You have all seen many examples of this type of advertising, the ads for special record offers, fishing reels, knives, kitchen utensils, etc. Manufacturers of these products have supplied the radio and TV stations with the ad materials. The station will then run the ad, ask the audience to send money for the product to their station, deduct a commission (usually 50% per order), and send the remainder along to the manufacturer of the product together with the name and address of the person who bought. The manufacturer then ships his product direct to the consumer. This is per order advertising. It is available because radio and TV stations have nothing more to sell than air time. If they have periods of time that are not sold, it is worthwhile for them to speculate on PO or PI advertising.

Per Inquiry advertising, obviously, is where you pay a set fee for every name that the station generates for you.

Whether or not these types of advertising are feasible or economical for you will depend on your market area and the price and drawing power of your prints. There is only one way to find out the answer to this question – test it. Start out slowly. If it works then increase a little at a time. If it fails then drop it and look for another angle.

THE BALANCE OF ADVERTISING – COST VERSUS RESPONSE

The most important question for any product is: "Does it pay to advertise?" Because of the limited market for costly art prints, this must be a question that you seriously consider.

Second, you are not in all likelihood starting out with a large bankroll to absorb your tests and mistakes. It is therefore extremely important for you to be cautious about spending money for any type of exposure unless you can justify the expense or are prepared for zero response or response at a loss. If you need any more encouragement on this point just keep in mind the numerous artists and writers who have starved while their work went on after their deaths to be worth a fortune.

I can only stress again that how a product is marketed is often more important to its success than the product itself. The biggest pitfall is to run out of money and be out of business before the product has time to catch on.

Just be cautious.

PAYING MONEY FOR ADVERTISING

Once you have received a reasonable amount of exposure for yourself and your art prints, it may be worthwhile considering spending money for advertising and other direct-to-the-consumer promotions.

The first question to ask yourself is: "Is there a market?" The answer to this is how well your prints have sold. If you have had success with your art dealers, architects, businesses, industries, etc., then chances are there are other people out there who would like to own your work.

The advantage of advertising is that it gets your sales force in front of a larger number of people without taking up a large amount of your time. Until now, a great deal of your time and effort has been required to set up your operation and test various markets for your work. If you can now set up a successful advertising campaign, you will be able to make many sales without ever directly confronting the customer. But if your prints have not sold well, don't advertise. At least not yet.

If your prints have just not moved then chances are the problem lies not in the buyer but in the seller. This means it is time for you to start asking yourself a number of questions: "Is the price too high? Are people not interested in buying this kind of prints? Is there something wrong with my preparation? Is there something wrong with my sales presentation?" There are many questions you can ask. Once you find the answer to the ones that cost you sales, it is time to move on to the next step.

There are basically several different types of advertising that we are not going to discuss here. What we are interested in is direct response advertising.

This includes: People sending you money for prints. People requesting further information on your prints. People coming down to your studio or shop to look at your prints.

Of these three, the two that will probably get you the most sales for your advertising dollar are the last two. If you ask people to send money directly for one of your prints, you will either sell them or lose them. Chances are you will lose more customers than you will sell. Also, potential customers for other prints not shown might be lost forever.

People who send in a request for more information are excellent potential buyers. Because of the high cost of advertising we simply cannot afford to run large ads. This means that we have a very limited amount of space to tell our story, show our prints and make our sale. If, on the other hand, we gear our ad to get interested parties to respond by mail, phone, or coming in, then we have the opportunity to give them enough additional information to make our sale.

Advertising, like successful publicity, should generate interest in your prints and initiate a response from interested parties. The actual sale will be made in your follow up. This may be done with a brochure, a sales letter, phone call, or even an appointment to show people your work at their homes, offices, or in your studio.

Obviously, the best time to advertise is along with any other publicity currently running on your work or on the subject of art — preferably art photographs. The publicity serves to give people an awareness that you and your art exist. The ad draws them into a response. Your follow-up gives you a solid shot at a sale. Without proper timing, the effectiveness of your advertising dollars will be severely weakened.

Let's say there is a major local art show scheduled that is due to draw a lot of people. If your work is entered, it's a good time to work at getting some publicity. You should approach both the editorial and advertising staff of the local newspapers. If editorial shows an interest in running a feature tie-in on your work and the upcoming show, this is great. If they are reluctant, don't give up. This is where you use some of the same business leverage everyone else uses from time to time. Let the ad staff know that you are planning on running one or several ads in conjunction with the show. Discuss some pre-show advertising, during and right at the end. Mention that you also think you have some really unique photos or ideas concerning photography as art. Be sincere and try to establish a rapport. Let them know that you are very serious about photographic art.

Try to convince them that an editorial feature on your work would have great news value and would help you a lot in spreading the word. If you can convince them, they may be able to encourage the editorial staff to run a story along with the ad. If you do run ads in this manner they must contain a sense of urgency. After all, the public in general is not going to have the facts about you and your photography in front of them again for some time. You must monopolize on this fact before you lose your edge and people forget about you again.

Gear your ad for people to write or call you for more information. Invite them to a special showing at your studio with beverages and snacks. Make them feel that you have something special or mysterious that they must see now. If necessary, let them know that you have some special prices on some otherwise expensive merchandise, or offer them a special package they can't ignore.

Motivating people is the name of the game in any kind of sales or advertising. If you are advertising locally, you will find that the ad representatives for papers, radio and TV stations, and other media will be more than happy to help you with various angles, copy preparation, sales ideas, etc. Take this help sincerely and try to learn from everyone you can. Just be cautious not to be caught up in their sales pitch. If you get too eager you may wind up buying more advertising than you need. Then you will have problems.

If you must, approach advertising agencies or copywriters for bit work. All of us have our limitations. There are definitely times when it will be cheaper in the long run for you to pay a few dollars for some needed copywriting or layout services. If you botch up your own ad, you may end up throwing a good idea away.

There are any number of good national art-oriented magazines and other publications. Art News for one has about the largest circulation of art-oriented readers. Remember, ad costs can really start adding up as you try to reach larger circulations of special interest groups. I would not even suggest you think about large expensive ads nationally unless you have a well established name, excellent collateral materials and a solid record of sales behind you.

Speaking of which, (if you haven't already figured it out) the whole object of advertising is to sort through the large numbers of uninterested parties for those select few who are interested in the type of product you have for sale. Once you have found the most efficient and least expensive way to reach these people, you have succeeded in the first goal of advertising.

CLASSIFIED ADVERTISING

If your collateral materials are strong enough to sell prints by themselves, you might consider classified advertising. Classifieds are an inexpensive way of reaching a large number of people at one time. You will have a very limited amount of room to state your message, so keep it brief and to the point.

> PHOTOGRAPHIC ART. A unique selection of limited edition photographs by local photographer (or nationally known — specialize in your own particular skill) Details: 2101 Stover, Ft. Collins, CO 80521.

The object of a good classified is to get people's interest, arouse their curiosity, inform them of your basic product, and motivate them to respond to your ad. You are paying by the word so keep it brief. Never ask for money in a classified unless your product speaks for itself, is priced low, and is virtually unavailable elsewhere. Even in these cases, it is still better to get people to respond first, then sell them with an informative sales letter or well-illustrated brochure or flyer.

OTHER WAYS OF OBTAINING LEADS

Most of the advertising, publicity, and promotional ideas we have been discussing are designed to get us 'leads'. These leads – names and addresses of people who have shown a genuine interest in our art photography – constitute the backbone of our sales to the public.

Large, sales-oriented companies use many different methods to generate leads. Sometimes, they will run contests for exciting prizes. To enter you must give your name and address and a lead is born. Other promotions include giving away free gifts (premiums) for responding to ads for more information about a product. Again, leads.

A lot of these kind of lead generating promotions are worthless for your little business. They work mostly on heavy volume and consumer-oriented products. Your product is specialized so you want quality leads, not volume leads.

One inexpensive way you can generate good leads is to put a reply coupon on a single page flyer describing some of your work. Have these flyers available at art shows, at dealers, or anywhere else where the kind of people you are interested in might congregate. If they are interested enough to cut out the coupon, fill out an envelope and put a stamp on it, then they are probably good prospects for your product.

DIRECT MAIL

One of the most effective sales vehicles I know is direct mail. It is not as personal, perhaps, as meeting someone in person or talking to him over the phone, but it has many advantages over other methods of approaching potential clients.

First of all, you can reach people at their leisure and on their own ground – their homes or offices. You have plenty of room to inform and show people your product. You can take all the time you need to prepare your sales materials – whether they be brochures, flyers or a direct personal letter.

If you are responding to leads, you should let people know it on the outside of your envelope: 'Enclosed is the material you requested about Fred Nelson's exciting Photography'. Many people are shy of direct mail and may neglect to open your envelope unless you let them know this is something they sent for and are expecting.

Let's talk for a minute about direct mail and privacy. You should not be shy about sending people mail concerning your product, especially if it is direct and tasteful. I feel sorry for people who object to receiving 'junk' mail. Most direct mail you get is a direct result of your own efforts: at some time in the past you indicated that you are a member of a special interest group. If you are an architect, you will probably receive information about new building structures and products related to your skills. In fact, if you purchased this book through the mail, it was because you had done something at one time or another to show your interest in photography or photographic art.

Personally, I look forward to my junk mail. It gives me a free opportunity to find out about new products and services. Sure I get some things that are completely off base. But if something doesn't interest me, I can simply throw it away – unopened, if I like. Can you say the same about TV? How many offensive or unrelated messages do you have pumped into your home nightly?

There are many ways to get reasonably qualified names for your direct mail campaign. It is possible that you can swap names and addresses with one of your interior designers, art dealers and the like. Because both of your clients have similar interests and needs, chances are good that they may have an interest in your product.

Another idea would be to put together a joint mailing. You and an interior designer or art dealer can each work up a flyer or brochure for your own products and services. Package them together in the same envelope and mail them to prospective clients. By running a joint campaign you will not only be able to split costs on postage, but you will probably get a larger percentage return because of the wider product selection available.

Look around for other people who may be mailing the kind of clients you are looking for.

Commercial lists can be rented. This can be done on both a local and a national level. Let's say there is a publication called

Art Buyers. The people who subscribe to this magazine make an average income of $40,000 to $80,000 a year. They are a select group of individuals from all over the country who have one thing in common – they buy art for pleasure and investment. Certainly, if you could get your hands on a mailing list of these specialized people, it would be a great help to you in your direct mail campaign. After all, you might have to mail to a hundred people interested in art before you find one that is a regular art buyer.

In a case like this, it would not hurt to write to the magazine and request information concerning the availability of their subscription list. It is best if you include an outline of your proposed campaign with this request. Chances are their list will be available for $30 to $40 per thousand names. These can be supplied to you on labels which will adhere directly to your envelopes.

It is important to remember that you only rent a list, you do not buy it. You may use it just once for the fee you paid. If people respond to your promotion, you may use their names for any purpose you desire. Keep in mind, however, that the seller of the list will include some bogus names which return your offer to his offices. This practice serves two purposes. First, it enables him to make sure you are using the list for legitimate purposes. Second, it assures him that you do not copy his list for use later, or sell it to someone else without permission.

I mentioned earlier that there are countless ways to launch successful mail campaigns. As always, be cautious. Start out small until you have proven your list and the material you are selling. Mail to a limited audience. The closer you can come to finding groups that already have an interest in art photography, the better chance you have that your campaign will succeed.

Be goal oriented. Organize your thoughts and your campaign. Don't haphazardly try to sell half the material you have ever produced. Be specific. Pick on a particular product, package or idea. If you sell this idea well, people will respond.

Direct mail is especially effective on a local or regional basis.

Here's an idea that can work for you. Let's assume that you have made one or more successful contacts with industry and have already sold one or more on the 'corporate story' idea we discussed earlier. Now that you have broken the ice, direct mail can gather momentum for you and reach a greater number of potential new accounts with similar businesses and industries.

Whenever your photographic art is used to decorate you should make every effort to document such use. Get permission from business owners to photograph their offices and conference rooms where your prints are hanging. Try to get shots that feature your work while, at the same time, showing how it is used effectively in the overall decoration of the room.

If you have managed to sell prints to the industry account — especially if their decoration includes both your stock prints and 'corporate story' photographs — make sure your original agreement guarantees you the right to take pictures of your work once it is hanging in their offices, lobbies, etc. Let them know in advance that you will be using some of these photos to advertise your service to other clients.

Once you have good photos showing your work in action, get together a list of similar industries and businesses where you think interest can be generated in your product. In most cases the yellow pages from surrounding areas will do the trick. Or write to the Chamber of Commerce in areas that interest you: ask for a list of local businesses and industries. They will be glad to comply.

Next, put together a 'corporate story' promotion geared directly towards industry and business. Include several optional standard packages in the event the other idea does not interest them. Because each corporate story project will differ, there is no need to put in charges or fees for your shooting into the original letter. Wait until you have made personal contact before you discuss exact money details.

The backbone of your promotion will be the business letter. Your business letter should outline what you have done and what you would like to do for them. Like any good business or sales letter it should be direct and brief but generate enough enthusiasm in your idea to make the reader want to respond. The purpose of this business letter is to get them interested in having you do some photographic art for them. Tell them that prices are available on request. Better yet, suggest to them that you would like to get together with them on the phone or in person to discuss their specific needs. Remember, a personal appointment is the most effective. If it means a long trip, try to set up several appointments in the same area over a one or two day period.

Included with your letter should be a flyer or similar promotional piece which illustrates how your photographic art has been used under similar conditions. This should consist of the photos you took showing your work in action. Include captions under the photos describing the setting and particular problems or unique applications you were faced with. You should also write some good descriptive copy which explains the philosophy or concept of decorating with photographic art and its wide range of applications. If you have prepared any other brochures (especially color) that show your photography, include these in the package as well.

There are many ways to use direct mail both to initiate new business and to close sales. Use your imagination and you will see opportunities all around you.

OTHER SALES VEHICLES

There are countless other ways to sell your work directly to the public.

Airport booths are now common for both lithographic prints and photography. They require a certain initial investment and upkeep but are very effective. People who do a lot of traveling generally have the kind of money it takes to collect art for pleasure and profit. Most important, airports, train stations, and other transportation centers have an incredibly high traffic of people. This means exposure to literally thousands of people each week. The more exposure the better chance you have of the right people seeing your work. Another aspect of travel that works to your advantage is waiting. People who have to spend more than one hour waiting in lobby areas are likely to get bored and look around for something of interest. A good airport display will get their attention.

Here are some things to keep in mind about any type of free standing display you might use:

1. They aren't free; you will pay rent for the space even if it is only five feet by five feet.
2. You will have to use your space very effectively. This means an attractive and functional display. It means that you will have to have some kind of rotating or collapsible panels which will accommodate ten to twenty samples of your work printed and matted as they are to be sold. It must be built solid so that you can easily remove and rotate your work from time to time. This will be necessary to get rid of images that are

not selling and replace them with fresh material.

3. You will need large quantities of 'take-one' sales material. These should co-ordinate with the prints on display. Black and white photos of the print will be useful. The color prints you have on display have already shown the public what they are buying. The 'take-one' will be essentially an order blank and address where people can send their checks or charge card numbers.
4. Pricing is important. You will be getting a lot of traffic but you will have to keep in their price range to make enough sales to justify cost, upkeep and rent on the display. If you want a lot of sales your prices will have to be in the $30-$40 range. Size of prints should be between 16x20 and 20x24. To make this work for you will mean volume printing and matting — again, a solid investment.
5. Test it first. Always test market any concept before you go into full production. This means break-even or very small profits until you can gear up your volume. Pick a high traffic area where the kind of people you wish to reach abound. This could be any of the transportation areas we discussed, shopping malls or even lobby areas of large hotels. If your booth is portable, you even can think of moving it regularly to places where people gather — sporting events, fraternal lodges, charity events, etc. In most of these cases, your rent can probably be a percentage of the action. If you know some charity groups that are holding plays, auctions, etc., approach them and offer your work for sale on a commission basis.

STORE DISPLAYS

A concept I have seen in action recently is a take off on the poster racks carried in many music stores, card shops, bookstores, etc. This is a tight display rack with unmounted 11x14 and 16x20 photographic prints which retail from $3.95 to $6.95. The volume required here is obvious but the concept seems to be working. One store I monitored over the past few months has moved a lot of prints. To make it work, you will need displays in a minimum of ten to twenty stores. Again, a solid investment.

WHOLESALING YOUR WORK

More than anything else, wholesaling your work takes a lot of good business sense. The markets available are virtually unlimited. What is important is your ability to come up with unique marketing ideas and co-ordinate your production so that you can still make solid profits while selling your work for very low prices.

We have already discussed pricing. Keep in mind that whomever you wholesale your work to will be assuming the burden of risk. Once he takes delivery of your prints, it will be up to him to find a retail outlet or direct sale for it. Therefore, he will have to be able to make a reasonable profit for his efforts and investment.

Keep in mind what your work will bring on a retail level. If it is going to sell for $40 then it is doubtful that you will be able to ask a wholesaler more than $10-$15. Remember, there are a lot of risks and expenses that will come out of the $25-$30 difference. Freight, packaging, advertising, commissions, salaries, store overhead, etc., are only a few.

There are a couple of different categories of wholesalers. Let's look at them one at a time.

CHAIN STORES

Chain stores are a good market and they can be cracked. They have the advantage of being able to buy large orders for all of their stores. The larger the order, the less it is going to cost you. Don't be afraid to contact them all – even biggies like Sears and Wards. You never know when you might make the right contact at the right time. To get in contact with the people you need, find out where the corporate offices are for each particular company and write to the Art Buyer or Home Furnishings Buyer. If the company has a catalogue, you can see if they carry art work similar to what you have in mind.

If possible, go into one of their stores and look around. See what kind of art they carry and in what price range. Ask sales personnel if they know who the buyer for the store is or where you can write to sell your work. If you have samples or a brochure with you, feel free to show it. First, the reaction you get to your work will help you continue to assess its salability. Second, if it impresses the sales people or the store manager, they will be even more willing to cooperate.

Your letter and presentation to the buyer should be first class. Like photo editors, they see a lot of professional, quality products and it will take a unique, dynamic approach to get their attention. By now, you should have picked up the basic philosophy of selling art prints. Apply it and you will make sales. The only major difference between selling your prints retail and wholesale is price and volume. You stand to make a lot more money if you can sell large quantities of prints. You may have to hit a lot of wholesalers before you make a hit – but one win will pay for your efforts.

ART WHOLESALERS

There are a variety of Art Wholesalers. The major ones supply finished art products to virtually every outlet in the world. These are people who deal in large lots of art. They buy in the thousands and then supply other, regional wholesale outlets.

Chances are pretty small that you will be able to crack these markets with photographic prints. However, that doesn't mean you can't sell your photography to them. Once you get some marketing experience under your belt and establish yourself as a top-flight photo artist, you should be able to approach these people with relative ease.

Instead of trying to sell them matted photographic prints, approach them with photo lithographs. Don't confuse these with posters. They are better quality and on heavier stock paper. To be successful, you will have to be able to supply the whole package – prints, frames and mats if necessary.

A local printer will not help you much here. Write to several major printers in large metropolitan areas. Outline your project. Ask them for quotes on separations and full-color press runs of 1,000, 5,000, 10,000, and 25,000. In most cases these printers will be able to put you in touch with large frame houses that can mass produce framing and other preparations necessary to produce your finished product.

Once you have a firm quote on the whole project and have figured in your profit margin, then approach the art wholesaler. Have the framer prepare two or three samples using your photographic prints. You can then explain to the wholesaler that the final work will be on a lithograph.

Finding the names of major printers and wholesalers in your region of the country is not that difficult. Your public library will have yellow pages for most of the major metropolitan areas. Other wholesalers are listed in Artist's Market. Both Photographer's Market and Artist's Market can be ordered through your local bookstore.

You will also find that most metropolitan areas have several regional art wholesalers. Try to set up an appointment and meet with them personally. If you have done your homework, you should be able to make some sales. Remember, two or three small wholesalers will result in the same kind of orders as one major wholesaler. Be persistent.

MAIL ORDER CATALOGUES

There are currently several hundred direct mail gift catalogues on the market. You probably receive some of them. Ask your friends and neighbors to borrow any they get. If you want to find out just how many there are, write to each catalogue you can find and tell them that you would like to be on their mailing list. Within a month or two you will be getting catalogues from everyone. Most of the major catalogues have several product lines and the others will be quick to sell your name and address to the competition.

Contacting gift catalogues is fairly simple. Write to the president or buyer: their names should be near the front of the catalogue. Send them color samples of your work (with return postage and packaging). Outline your wholesale rates, delivery times, etc. Try to give them as much background material as you can, how well your prints have sold, to what types of people, etc. If they are interested, they will respond and you can begin the real negotiations.

One of my first major sales came from a gift catalogue. I was just sending the color brochures at random to various contacts I knew. One of the gift catalogues we received was laying around the office, so I sent them a brochure, too. Four days later I received a letter from the president of the company saying that she was excited about my work. Like an idiot, I flew fifteen hundred miles to meet with her personally. When I got there no one remembered I had an appointment (I set it up the day before with a hasty phone call). Luckily, I managed to catch her during her lunch break. I didn't have any wholesale prices or any other data prepared and it could have been a disaster. Fortunately, I had a pocket calculator and a price catalogue from my lab. We hashed it out and settled on a hundred prints of one of my limited editions. I learned to be better prepared after that.

Incidentally, gift catalogues and similar publications are good prospects for your limited editions. Art wholesalers will be interested only in non-limited material at the beginning. Until they have established a strong market for your work they will not be interested in small, more expensive quantities of your work. Once they are handling at least six or more of your images, they may consider an exclusive limited edition for the retail outlets that move most of your work. The same applies to department stores and other commercial outlets. Once they have established a demand for your work, people will be looking for it. Some of them will actually be collecting it. This is the time to capitalize with limited editions.

Several other ideas about catalogue-type markets. The catalogue departments of major chain stores like Sears, Wards, and the like, are completely separate from the retail store outlet. In many cases they are actually in competition with the store. This means separate buyers and management for both. In other words, submit your material to both the retail store buyer and the catalogue department buyer. If you miss a sale with one you might make it with the other. Also, many of the magazines put out by major credit cards (Carte Blanche) or airlines have gift sections. Every one of these is worth approaching.

CUSTOM LIMITED EDITIONS – PAY AS YOU GO

I have found that the practice of producing custom limited editions is by far the most sensible way to begin selling your line of limited edition prints.

The traditional way to produce a limited edition is to produce the entire set at one time. Certainly this is the least expensive per print if you are going to sell an edition of fifty or more. In fact, it is absolutely necessary for artforms like woodcuts, lithographs and the like. If they printed the edition at different times, it would be very difficult to get the dyes the same or maintain a certain quality.

A custom limited edition photograph is done exactly this way, printed one at a time either before or after the sale. In this case, the image itself is limited to the number of prints in the edition.

Yes, there will be some color difference, but in many ways, these prints have the possibility of becoming even more valuable because they are not mass-produced. The important thing is to print a strip print at the very beginning that you can use for the duration to match against. And by printing them one at a time, chances are that you will be able to have even better quality control.

One of the things I personally like about this method is the flexibility it offers. To begin with you can print your photographs different sizes. Thus, if someone wants to go all out and buy a mural he would have something definitely unique and thus more valuable. This technique allows you to cater to many different people's tastes while still limiting the production of prints. Naturally, this type of production makes it even more important to keep exact records of what has been printed, what size, and where it went.

Another thing that becomes possible is cutting off production on weaker prints. If you had planned an edition of fifty but were only able to sell ten or fifteen over a two year period, you might wish to close out the edition, destroy the original and call it quits with that particular image. With the edition closed out, those prints that do exist will then be able to float up in value. If you do cut off the edition you must be certain that all buyers are informed and that there is public access to your records concerning the edition.

The only disadvantage of this system is your cost per unit. You will have to sell your prints for more or receive a smaller profit. Still, you will have saved a great deal of money up front and reduced your risk considerably.

You might also note that selling the edition this way will not really prevent you from making occasional volume runs within an edition. If you land a larger account and wholesale ten or twenty prints, print them at your best price, but make a note on your records for that edition that X number of prints were sold to Z corporation and were printed *en masse.* If someone wants to get sticky down the road as to whose print is worth more, they can resort to your records.

DESTROYING THE ORIGINAL

Unfortunately, this must be done.

I have fought the idea for a long time, but it is one tradition that must be honored. True, as a photographer there are many other ways that you can make money from a photograph. Just because it is one of your limited editions in no way prevents it from being published in other forms. In fact, the exposure will do the print a world of good. While such media as magazine covers, or articles illustrating your artwork are definite goes, you should avoid any imitation artwork such as posters, etc.

When the edition is printed, you must destroy the original. Even though you have protected your buyers with authorization sheets, etc., there really isn't anything to prevent someone else from getting hold of your originals after your death, or stealing them and printing illegal copies. Besides, a public destruction of the negative is a declaration that the edition is officially closed. Often, it is not until this declaration that your work begins to appreciate in value.

So destroy your originals. Make a scene of it, verified by your notary or some other public official. And destroy all originals or dupes that have been produced. Do it right and it will be to your advantage in the end.

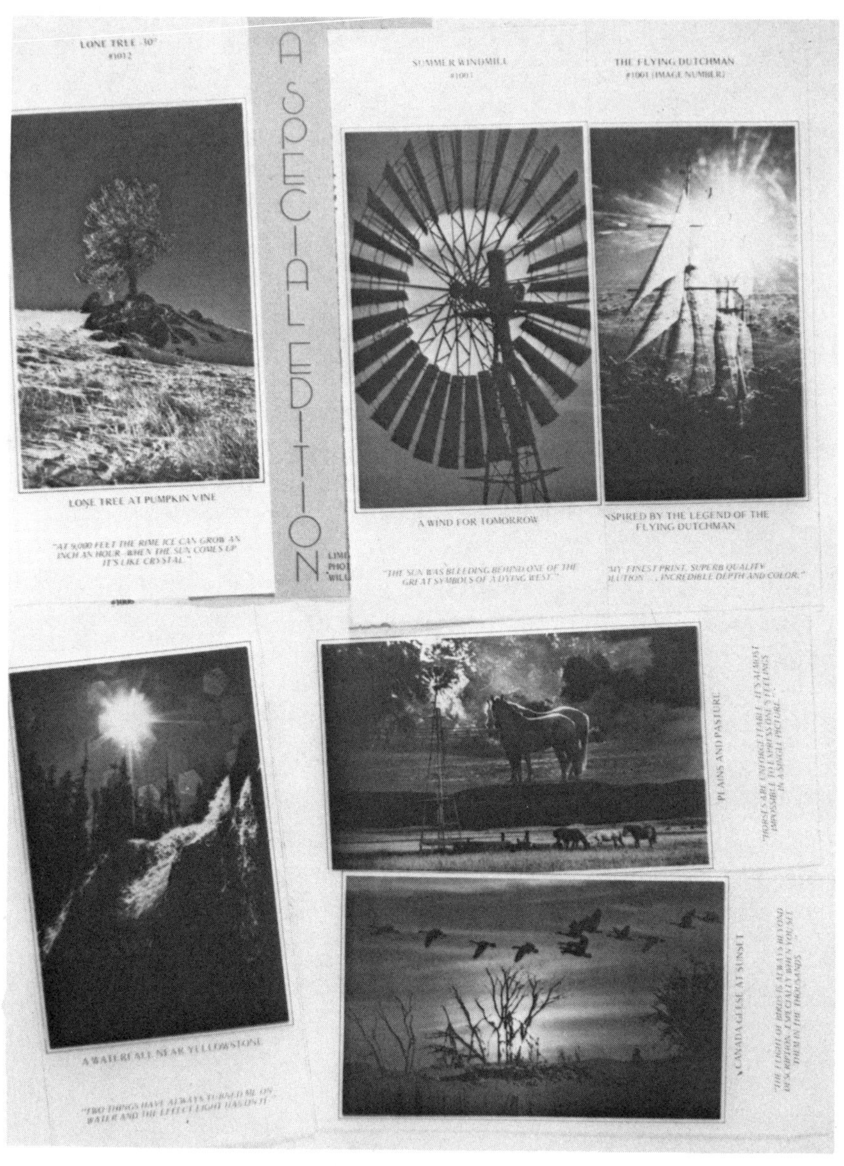

On pages 67 through 73 Eastman discusses the full-color brochure used to sell his limited edition prints. Shown in this photograph are the cover of the brochure and some of its ten color illustration. The size of the brochure is 4″x9″ so it fits a standard #10 business envelope.

SECTION IV

COLLATERAL MATERIALS

Collateral materials include anything which you print to assist you in the sale of your Art Photographs. These include stationery, brochures, flyers, sales materials, order blanks, biography sheets, and anything else you require for a single promotion or as a part of your total sales package.

HANDOUTS AND FLYERS

The flyer is an extremely useful tool. It is inexpensive and simple. Most of the time it can be printed on one side of a single page. Flyers are produced for one reason, to communicate one or several brief ideas. If you are having a showing of your work, several hundred copies of a flyer can be produced at a 'quick printer' for less than $10. If you are at a show (or somewhere else where art oriented people have gathered) you might wish to prepare a brief, informative flyer or handout about your work. At the end of it you can extend an invitation for people to visit your studio to see more of your work or call you for further information.

Flyers are seldom taken home to be read at leisure so the message must be brief and to the point. The average flyer should consist of a maximum of three elements:

1. THE HEADLINE. This is your gripper statement. It should instantly let your reader know what the body of the flyer is all about. It must get their attention if you wish them to read your message. Here are some samples: "AN INVITATION TO A SPECIAL PHOTOGRAPHIC ART EXHIBIT." "EXPERIENCE THE ART OF JOHN WAXMAN." "SPECIAL SALE FOR PHOTOGRAPHIC ART BUFFS". Obviously, there are dozens of angles.

The headline is your way of gearing people towards your specific promotion.

2. BODY COPY. Your body copy must be brief and to the point as well. People will not have the patience to wade through prose and flowery descriptions to find out what you are trying to tell them. "A special photographic art exhibit is now being held for a limited time by John Waxman at his studio in Clarence Heights. Members of the art community are invited to attend, as well as private parties interested in the popular, dramatic art of John Waxman. Etc." Get your message across as economically as possible. If you need to include additional biographical information limit yourself to the most important points. Don't include information that is irrelevant or of little interest to what you are trying to accomplish.
3. CLOSING STATEMENT. Your closing statement must motivate. If the purpose of the flyer is to sell something, the closing statement must ask for the sale. It must tell people how much and where to send the money. If you are inviting people to a showing or asking them to call or write for additional information, the closing statement must make this clear and motivate people to do exactly this.

BIOGRAPHY SHEET

Another type of flyer that you will find very useful is a biography sheet. In the absence of a formal brochure, the biography sheet is a valuable tool to have available at places where your art is on display or for sale.

The biography sheet is a sales tool, not a sales piece. It should include any pertinent background information on you and your photography. A list of your most important credits should be worked into the body copy casually in a way that lets people know who you are and what you have done without trying to openly impress them or brag. You may wish to include a small black and white photo of yourself and possibly a sample or two of your work. The main object of a biography sheet is to inform people and answer some of their questions about you and your photography. Remember, if people do buy your work, they are going to want to tell others about it. If they know some juicy tidbits about the photographer who produced the work, they will pass these along in the conversation. It makes them feel good because they know something about you, and it helps you because others are getting first-hand information without your putting in any additional time and effort.

Again, a biography sheet is not meant to sell by itself. It should, however, include an address where people can write for more information about your work. If the biography sheets are going to be used mostly in places where your work is for sale, you can leave a blank for the dealer's name and address.

THE BROCHURE

The brochure is the workhorse of your art print business. It must be able to tell the whole story in your absence and sell your prints by itself.

There are many forms of brochures, many sizes, colors and most importantly — *costs!*

There isn't time here to educate those of you who know absolutely nothing about printing, layout and copywriting. Your local printer will be able to help you with your specific needs, and we will cover some basics. Once you have an understanding of what you need to accomplish, the details can be worked out. I suggest that you be cautious and seek information anywhere you can get it. Once you have a solid working knowledge of the basic elements and the way printers work, you can progress more surely.

The best place to start is at your travel agent. No, this isn't the time to throw up your hands and leave the country. Travel agents and Chambers of Commerce, however, are excellent places to pick up free brochures to study. The same goes for your local camera store.

You will notice that most brochures are not formally bound 'booklets', but consist of a single page cleverly folded into many pages. Study carefully every brochure you can find. Notice how they present their copy and lay out their photographs. Once you get a feeling for what is going on, you will find putting together your own brochure not that difficult.

Before we go further, there is that one thing I would like to talk about again. This is cost. A color brochure can be extremely expensive. In fact my own brochure was the biggest expense involved in gearing up my limited edition sales.

A black and white brochure will take a maximum of two negatives for the printer. One is a line negative which picks up all of your single-tone art work, the headlines and all written copy.

The second negative is a halftone which is required to reproduce any multi-tone art such as photographs. Halftones are comprised of a series of dots which result when your photograph or other art work is re-photographed through a screen. If you have never seen a halftone before, take a magnifying glass to any magazine or newspaper. You will see the dots everywhere. In the dark areas they seem to be more dense. The light areas contain the same number of dots, but much smaller. A halftone simply keeps the detail in your photographs. Without them, the photograph would lose all its subtle shading and be as black and white as the type.

The two negatives are put together onto the final offset plate which works like a stencil, accepting ink from the press and transferring it to the paper.

Color printing is much more complicated. Whereas black and white printing will require only one press run for each side of the page, full-color printing will take four complete press runs. This alone will increase the cost of your job four times. The most expensive part, however, is often your separations. These are the individual negatives (usually four per photograph) that must be made for each color press run. Color separations generally cost from $50 to $125 per photograph. This is a separate expense from your typesetting, printing, folding and binding.

As you might have guessed, the larger quantity of brochures you order the lower the price. In the hundreds of thousands even the most complicated color printing can be reduced to several cents apiece. Chances are pretty good that you won't be wanting any more than a few hundred to a thousand brochures to start out with.

Your first economical quantity of any printed work (black and white or color) is a thousand copies. Most printers figure any job for a minimum thousand run. If the customer wants less, they generally only deduct the cost of the paper. If a thousand copies of a black and white brochure are going to cost you $250 you will probably find that five hundred will cost you $225. So get a quote for several quantities and then decide what you can justify. If you are going to need more in just three months, it is best to print them now.

SET-UP COST

Your set-up cost is expensive. The type has to be set, the negatives made and stripped onto the plate. Most of the labor to be done must be finished before the first press run. You will find that a reprint later on will save you at least one-third of the initial cost because the set-up is already completed.

In the case of a color job this can be very significant. My first color brochure cost about $2,200 for 5,000, a per unit cost of 44 cents. That's expensive. It would have been worse for a thousand. In this case, the color separations alone cost $800, a one-time cost. On a second press run of 5,000 my cost was cut nearly in half because all of the labor and set-up was done and the plates were already to go to the presses.

GETTING LAYOUT HELP

If you are not experienced in layout or copywriting, it is possible to get some help for little or no charge. Often a local printer will be able to give you some of his time and advice. Many larger printers have an in-house staff to do this kind of work, but there are some things that you can't expect to get free, like art work. If you do need help, simply ask what it will cost. If they want your job bad enough they will probably agree to help you up to a point for nothing.

Another source to try is a printing broker or an ad agency. These people receive a 15% commission from the printer on every job they take in. Once you give them your job, they will take over all the responsibilities of seeing that it is done correctly and on time. If you need just a little help, they will often lend a hand at no charge to get your job.

BLACK AND WHITE OR COLOR?

The question still remains – which way should you go?

If you are supplying your brochures to an unattended booth where your photos are on display, black and white will easily do the job. Even if you could get a brochure in color for 20 cents apiece, it is still too expensive to leave around for some kids to walk off with. The same applies if you are handing out brochures at a show where your work is on display or leaving some at various dealers where your photos are for sale. Black and white may not be a very dramatic way to show your prints, but if people have been exposed to the originals, they will probably not need expensive color brochures to convince them to buy.

If, on the other hand, you are going to be doing a lot of remote promotions for your prints, you should give some serious consideration to a color brochure. Just because mine was expensive doesn't mean that you can't produce one for less that is just as effective. Your brochure is like a business card – you want people to keep it so that it will be on hand if they ever do need your prints or services. My brochure was directly responsible for several assignments and major contracts long before I sold enough prints to justify its cost. A brochure that dramatically illustrates your work can be a great door opener for many of your projects. It can also supply you with a kind of instant credibility.

The decision for black and white or color is up to you. Talk with your local printer and get some cost estimates before you make the final decision. Try to keep your costs down until you have established a definite market for your prints.

SIZE

In the majority of cases your brochure should be able to fit into a regular #10 business envelope. This is not only convenient but a very economical and fast way to mail out materials to prospective clients. My experiences show that anything larger than a #10 – even if it is clearly marked 'first class' – always takes a day or two longer to go through the postal system.

You will notice that many of the fold-out brochures you have picked up will fold out into different sizes and shapes. Even though these might look like they have been done randomly in regards to their size, this is not the case. Printers must buy their paper in standard sizes. Most brochures that are well planned will take into account these standard sizes and will be designed so that a maximum number can be cut out of the sheet without any waste. If you do come up with an odd size without consulting your printer first, chances are you are going to spend a lot of money for paper that is thrown away or cut up into note pads.

THE ELEMENTS OF A GOOD BROCHURE

THEME. Whether your brochure is to serve as an introduction to you and your work in general or is designed to sell a specific set of limited edition or art prints, it needs to have a definite theme.

It is not difficult to see that the goal of a photographer producing a color brochure on his wedding photography is to motivate parents and couples to come to him for their wedding photographs. But an effective brochure must have more than a few nice photos and a price list. It needs cohesion in the form of an underlying theme.

In the opening statement of my brochure I outline the purpose of a Special Edition. By informing the reader about the basic details of my offer, I set the stage for the photographs that follow.

The wedding photographer would probably use his opening statement to introduce his reader to the purpose and long range value of wedding memories through fine photography. At the same time, he should begin to introduce himself – his personality and his attitudes and approach to wedding photography.

The same would apply if you produced a corporate story brochure. The theme of the brochure is the corporate story. This theme should be incorporated everywhere, even as you inform your reader about the specifics of your proposal. Like the wedding photographer, your personality and approach should also show through.

In my brochure, I was able to continue the theme throughout by adding bits and pieces of superfluous prose beneath the titles of each photograph. Although the scenes and settings were often entirely different, the photos maintain their impact and cohesion through the personality of the photographer and the prose tie-in.

Once you have decided on the photos you wish to use look for a theme tie-in that will help hold your project together as a single unit.

BIOGRAPHICAL INFORMATION. Every personalized sales piece on art photographs should contain some biographical information. We have discussed credibility and the many other advantages of this before. When it comes to spending larger amounts of money, people want to know whom they are dealing with. The same applies whether you are a surgeon or a photographer: people need to be able to put their confidence in you.

Whether you include your biographical and credibility information along with your opening statement or separately is up to you. It should include, however, the answers to at least these three questions: "Who are you?"; "What have you done?"; and "Why are you doing it?"

DISPLAYING YOUR PHOTOGRAPHS. How your photographs are displayed is extremely important. If you feel you are completely inept at any kind of photo layout, spend more time looking at those other brochures. Don't copy their ideas, but modify some of them to fit your approach. Remember as well that many brochures and other publications use photography only as a kind of secondary illustration. They crop and jam in photos to fit in and around their copy. Photography is your business, so your photographs should dominate. Move the copy around to fit the photos, not vice versa.

There are several basic ideas to keep in mind depending on your theme and other factors. In my particular brochure, I wanted to show off each photo as a separate art print. For this reason, I gave each one an equal display on a page of its own.

If all of your photos are of the same subject matter — wildlife, close up, scenics, abstracts, couples, etc., you may wish to feature certain images more than others. This would be especially easy to do if you were using the single-page, fold-out type brochure. On an open fold you could feature one or two of your most dramatic photos for the single purpose of impact. Then, inside, include your body copy along with the remainder of your photos tastefully arranged.

As usual, the possibilities are unlimited. But the more unique and interesting your brochure is by itself, the more people will want to pick it up and read it without any invitation or reason, and the greater the chances are that your brochure will serve its purpose — to sell your photographic art.

ORDER BLANK. Your accountant will probably tell you this is the most important part of the brochure — and he's right! Without making it simple and convenient for people to order your work you are wasting your time and money.

Your order blank should include all the information on prints, sizes, costs, etc. that is necessary. Take a moment and look at my brochure. One side of the page gives all of the above order information. The other side asks for the order. We have included the name and address, quantity, image and size. These are the obvious things.

The office code at the top right is for the purpose of letting us know where the order came from. If the brochure was one of those we left in a booth we might code it 'B' for booth. The same would apply if we handed out brochures at an art show or responded to an ad, etc. Each of the brochures is coded prior to going out to help us gauge our response to each promotion. You will find a code on the brochure in front of you. This is because this book will have a secondary impact on the sale of my photos. Experience has shown me that professional photographers who are interested in producing their own limited edition photos are also susceptible to buying mine. In fact, one out of fifty of you will probably order from the enclosed brochure. Why? 1) You like my photos. 2) My brochure and this book are helping establish my credibility and serious interest in photography as an art form. 3) Because I am a salesman as well as a photographer. No matter how sincere I am and how much I want to help you sell your photography, I still want to sell mine. You should do the same.

You should always arrange it so that people can use their Mastercard and Visa. This is easy to set up with your local banker and will be worthwhile in the long run. You will pay a percentage to the bank, but you will also make it possible for people to manage their own money. If people receive your brochure in the middle of the month and have to pay cash, chances are they will have to wait until payday. By then the odds of their placing an order are reduced by at least fifty percent. If they can't find the money in the budget then, you will have even a lesser chance of getting their order.

Remember, the object of sales is to motivate people to buy when they are at their peak interest in a product. Once they put aside the 'Buy Now' temptation, it becomes easier to postpone buying. Make it easy on your customers – use the bank cards. It will give you enough of a percentage in sales you would not otherwise get to justify the effort.

Offer them a guarantee. If you believe in your product, stand behind it. One of the primary reasons people hesitate to buy by mail is the fear of being taken advantage of. If you stand behind your product and tell them so, they will be more at ease and more likely to buy. If your product is good, chances are very slim that people will return it.

When you are replying to orders by mail make sure you insure your prints. One of my 20x24 Flying Dutchman was delivered bent in half by the postal system. It had 'PHOTOGRAPHS – DO NOT BEND' written all over it, but that made little difference.